THE LIBRARY OF HISTORY AND DOCTRINE

OUR LIFE IN CHRIST

THE LIBRARY OF HISTORY AND DOCTRINE

The aim of this international Library is to enable scholars to answer
questions about the development of the Christian tradition which are
important for an understanding of Christianity today

OUR LIFE IN CHRIST

J. K. S. REID
*Professor of Christian Dogmatics
in the University of Aberdeen*

Philadelphia
The Westminster Press

PRINTED IN GREAT BRITAIN

CONTENTS

PREFACE

IT is seventy years since the singular importance of the phrase 'in Christ' was brought to the notice of modern theology. During this time the fact of its importance has been widely accepted, and the contribution it makes to the understanding of St Paul's theology and in general of the Christian faith largely neglected. The attempt is made here to use the concept for interpreting the Christian Gospel.

When this is done, it becomes clear that a right statement of the Gospel must emphasize that the object of faith has absolute priority over our faith. The Gospel is not primarily concerned with faith. It is primarily concerned with that upon which faith reposes, the object that has faith as its proper correlate, the *kerygma* that arouses faith. The *opus Christi* has primacy over every and all *opus humanum* —even the *opus fidei*. Some of the problems that arise from this are here discussed.

While the argument is often academic, it is hoped that an evangelical and pastoral interest may also be served. Evangelical earnestness is always degenerating into a kind of *fideism*—the demand for faith and a reliance upon what faith thus aroused can do. No wonder, if it is thought that 'the old, old story' must simply be repeated in the old, old words. The keynote of Christianity, however, is not exhortation—not even exhortation to faith—but declaration: instead of fresh burdens, Christianity offers 'all joy and peace in believing'. Consideration of how our life may be said to be in Christ underlines this essentially evangelical principle.

The chapters of this book are, in slightly altered form, lectures given at Princeton Theological Seminary. The appointment to deliver there the Warfield Lectures for 1960 was a highly appreciated honour, and the association with the Seminary was unforgettably agreeable. It is true that Dr Warfield himself, at the 1890 Assembly of the Presbyterian Church, affirmed that the Westminster Confession unrevised 'suited him down to the ground'; true too that Charles Hodge when professor in the Seminary declared, with equal recklessness and pride, that 'a new idea never originated in this Seminary'. But it is many years since these sentiments were expressed, and even so the magnitude of the change that has meantime taken place in the theological atmosphere can nowhere be measured merely in years. Suffice it to say that the present writer looks back upon his stay at Princeton Theological Seminary with unmixed satisfaction, and for the members of the faculty, and not least for its Principal, Dr J. I. McCord, and for Professor G. S. Hendry, he will always cherish feelings of gratitude.

Aberdeen   J.K.S.R.

I

The Phrase 'in Christ'

1. The term 'Christian'

THE familiar term 'Christian' has achieved its universal currency in spite of origins that are dubious and equivocal. It appears three times in the New Testament. (i) In Acts 11.26, we are told that 'the disciples were called Christians first in Antioch'; (ii) in Acts 26.28, Agrippa is reported to have declared to St Paul whom he was judicially examining: 'Almost thou persuadest me to become a Christian'; (iii) in I Peter 4.16, the apostle, writing to communities throughout Asia Minor, urges that 'if any man suffer as a Christian, let him not be ashamed; but let him glorify God on this behalf'. From the context of the first passage, we learn that it was at Antioch that Barnabas introduced the converted Saul of Tarsus to his first experience of a community of the followers of Jesus, and in the fellowship of this church, the most considerable outside Jerusalem, the two of them lived for a full year. The date of this year-long sojourn cannot be exactly fixed, but it is probably to be placed earlier than the Herodian persecution of 44. The name, then, has been coined at least as early as ten years after the earthly career of Jesus ended. The second passage refers to a period some twenty years later. By this time the name is so well known in the circle of Roman officials at Caesarea as apparently to need no explanation or commentary. The third passage discloses the fact that a year or two later still, say 65 or 66, the name is familiar throughout Asia Minor.

Such evidence as there is shows that the followers of Jesus are not themselves to be credited with the invention of the name. The linguistic evidence of the earlier passage in Acts is inconclusive—'were called' ($\chi\rho\eta\mu\alpha\tau\iota\sigma\alpha\iota$) does not clearly indicate a name imposed by others rather than adopted for oneself. But in the later passage, when St Paul replies to Agrippa (Acts 26.29), it is noticeable that he declines to employ the term that has just been used; he prefers to substitute 'such as I am', and this avoidance may well be deliberate. In the third passage quoted, it is indeed a follower of Jesus who uses the term. But as it appears here, the phrase 'as a Christian' is paralleled by 'as a thief' and 'as a murderer'; and this is enough to show that 'the writer is speaking for a moment from the point of view of the heathen persecutor'[1] and borrowing the term from the charges brought against them by their accusers. In the absence of any other occurrences of the term, it must be concluded that the Christians themselves did not coin it.

Nor is there any good reason to suppose that the name was of Jewish invention. Elsewhere in the New Testament, the Jews appear to use two names to designate Christians. They are called 'the sect of the Nazarenes' (Acts 24.5) or simply 'this sect' (ἡ αἵρεσις, Acts 28.22), and St Paul acknowledges his own adherence to 'the way which [the Jews] call heresy' (Acts 24.14). It is not possible to regard the Jewish king Agrippa as a reliable mouthpiece of current Jewish modes of speech (Acts 26.28), and here he certainly represents Roman ideas to Romans in familiar Roman terms. Besides, it must be reckoned inherently improbable that the Jews would be inclined to refer to this new heretical group by a name which connected them even in irony with the Anointed One and the Messiah.

There is, however, no difficulty at all in supposing that the keen-witted populace of Antioch, already famous for their bestowal of nicknames,[2] should have been responsible for inventing the name of Christian.[3] And this supposition is confirmed by the evidence of Tacitus,[4] whose declaration, *quos vulgus Christianos appellabat*, indicates a common and popular term current for a long time by the year 64. It is safe to conclude that 'the name was first given to the worshippers of Jesus by the Gentiles'.[5] Even if doubts remain concerning the origin of name, it is scarcely possible to overlook the contemptuous significance it seems to bear. Agrippa's reference contains barely concealed scorn, while St Peter testifies that in the heathen mind 'Christian' is virtually equivalent to 'malefactor'.

---

[1] See S. C. Gayford's article 'Christian' in Hasting's *Dictionary of the Bible*, Edinburgh 1898, 385a.
[2] See *The Expositors's Greek Testament*, ad loc.
[3] But cf. *per contra HDB* new edition, where Otto Piper in an article on 'Christian' will maintain that the ending -os requires a Latin origin, whereas a Greek origin, e.g. in Antioch, would have supplied the ending -ios.
[4] *Ann.* xv. 44.
[5] Grimm-Thayer, *Greek-English Lexicon of the New Testament*, Edinburgh 1901, ad loc.

But, not for the only time in history,[1] a name given in dubious circumstances was to live down its disreputable origins, to become universally accepted and adopted, and to acquire the dignity of a title of honour. By way of the Ignatian Epistles,[2] from the time of Justin Martyr[3] onwards, the term 'Christian' had won this status.

But if Christians did not readily call themselves by the name in the New Testament, they did not lack terms by which to denote themselves. They called themselves 'the brethren' (Acts 14.2; 15.13; Rom. 16.14, etc.); 'the disciples' (Acts 11.26; 13.52; 20.30); 'the saints' (Rom. 16.15; I Cor. 16.1; Eph. 1.18, etc.); 'the faithful' (Acts 10.45; I Tim. 4.3, 12); men 'of the way' (Acts 9.2; 19.9, 23; 24.22). While the term 'Christian' remains almost purely nominal, these other phrases carry a considerable content. They do not merely denote, but also connote; they not only designate a group of people, but describe the group by certain characteristics. Putting the phrases together, we should know a good deal about what was meant in New Testament times by 'being a Christian', as we should now express it. The technical appellation is not used by Christians of themselves; but instead we have these various word-pictures of what a Christian was like.

2. St Paul's 'in Christ' and its origins

To this list of significant names, St Paul has the distinction of adding another. It too is not a mere name. For all its brevity, it is a descriptive term, all the more significant because it suggests a description at the most profound level. It is the simple phrase 'in Christ', with its equivalent 'in the Lord'. 'The formula which Paul most frequently used to describe the nature of the Christian man was that he was "in Christ".'[4] The present chapter will examine this phrase as it appears in St Paul's writings, with some reference to other books of the New Testament; and the aim of the chapters that follow will be to elicit its theological implications.

In 1892 Adolf Deissmann, then a *Privatdozent* in Marburg, published a small book entitled *Die neutestamentliche Formel 'in Christo*

[1] Cf. the nickname 'Quakers' given to the Friends by the Puritan magistrate, Gervase Bennett, at Derby in 1650, apparently borrowing the term from a sect who shivered and shook under religious excitement and were designated by it in 1647.

[2] *Rom.* 3.3; *Magn.* 4; *Eph.* 11.2; cf. *Mart. Polyc.* 3, 10, 12.

[3] See *Apol.* 1.4; *Dial. c. Trypho* 35; and also the *Didache* 12.4.

[4] W. D. Davies, *Paul and Rabbinic Judaism*, London 1948, 86.

Jesu'. Since this date, it has hardly been possible to write about St Paul's theology without reference to the phrase or reckoning with this monograph. Not all its statements and conclusions have gone unchallenged, but, if the assembled statistical data and nothing else are allowed to be true, the work demonstrates beyond all doubt the unusual prominence of the formula in the mind and thought of St Paul. The phrase assumes different forms. In the Pauline literature, the form most frequently occurring is ἐν Χριστῷ, with ἐν κυρίῳ a close second and ἐν Χριστῷ Ἰησοῦ some distance behind in the third place. With still less frequency occur the expressions ἐν αὐτῷ and ἐν ᾧ. But the notable fact emerges that in the Pauline corpus the phrase in one or other of its forms occurs no fewer than 164 times. To complete the picture, Deissmann calculates that the phrase occurs 24 times in the Johannine corpus (including the Apocalypse), only 8 times in Acts and 1 Peter, and nowhere else in the New Testament. Further, the phrase is entirely absent from the parts of the New Testament which are earliest or dependent on the earliest sources, i.e. the Synoptic Gospels. It makes a sudden appearance in the Pauline literature. The post-Pauline writings are all more or less influenced by it. While the frequency of its occurrence in St Paul compared with the rest of the New Testament is striking, within his writings themselves it appears with diminishing frequency in the three groups respectively into which historical investigation has divided them, the earlier Epistles, the imprisonment Epistles, and the pastoral Epistles. As Deissmann says,[1] the fact that the phrase occurs so often and makes its appearance with such suddenness cannot but arouse the keenest interest: the formula 'is really the characteristic expression of [St Paul's] Christianity'.[2]

The suddenness of its appearance raises the question of origin. Johannes Weiss[3] regards it as a pertinent question 'whether Paul himself created . . . the formula "in Christ", or has taken it over from some other source.' Contemporary religious modes of thought and feeling supply a possible source from which St Paul might be borrowing. Weiss[4] gives several examples of such expressions, of which one must here suffice: 'Come into my spirit and soul throughout my whole life, and do everything for me that my soul desires.

---

[1] *Die neutestamentliche Formel 'in Christo Jesu'*, Marburg 1892, 1 f.
[2] *Paul*, Eng. trs.[2], London 1926, 140.
[3] Johannes Weiss, *The History of Primitive Christianity*, Eng. trs., London 1937, vol. II, 465.
[4] Op. cit. 465 n. 18.

For you are I and I am you; what I say, may it always come to pass; for I have your name as an amulet in my heart; no swinging fist will ever overcome me; nor be able to withstand me, neither a spirit nor a demon, no occurrence, nor any other evil coming from Hades—for the sake of your name which I have in my soul.'[1] This is the authentic language of mysticism. That there is a Pauline mysticism need not at this point be disputed; but there is a wide difference between what is said here and the formula 'in Christ'. The expression 'in Christ' preserves a clear distinction between the individual and Christ in whom he is, and St Paul is never found saying, 'Christ is I and I am Christ'. This distinction is obliterated in the words quoted from heathenism, and the affirmation that it is only a 'name' that the individual has in his soul hardly amends the situation. Much the same thing has to be said about the other quotations which Weiss assembles. It follows that no clear case has been made out, at least so far, for a direct borrowing on the part of St Paul from the contemporary mystical literature. Weiss prudently concludes that the question he poses is not easy to answer. Deissmann, on the other hand, is bolder. After detailed discussion, he comes to the conclusion[2] that St Paul 'was the inventor of the formula, not in the sense of being the first to use ἐν with a personal singular, but in the sense that he employed an already existing idiom to form a new technical term'. The evidence as known can lead to no other conclusion.

But a further question has here to be faced. Granted that the phrase is characteristic of St Paul, and granted that for it he is not at least directly dependent upon non-Christian sources; may we suppose that it is a phrase current in the Christianity into which he was introduced? or is it at least representative of a concept elsewhere to be found in the New Testament? The two parts of the question have to be examined separately. As Deissmann has pointed out, the phrase occurs elsewhere in the New Testament only in Acts, I Peter and the Johannine corpus. There can be no question of St Paul being dependent on the last as the source from which he borrows the phrase. The probable dates for the composition of the other two books make it similarly impossible for St Paul to draw upon them. Besides, the phrase is used in these books sporadically, and its occurrences are little more than approximations to the way

---

[1] Quoted loc. cit. from Reitzenstein, *Poimandres*, 19 ff., from a prayer to Hermes.
[2] *Die nt Formel*, 70.

in which it is used by St Paul. The written documents of the New Testament give no ground for supposing that St Paul is borrowing from contemporary Christianity. The second part of the question, however, opens up quite a different range of possibilities. The phrase does not occur in the Synoptic Gospels, and there can therefore be no question of St Paul borrowing directly from their antecedents. It is, however, not so clear that some kind of equivalent is not there to be found. J. S. Stewart maintains[1] that 'it is at least possible that the idea comes from Jesus himself'. There is, he suggests, a hint of it for example in Matt. 18.20: 'Where two or three are gathered together in my name, there am I in the midst of them.' Evidence corroborative of this is to be found indirectly in the Fourth Gospel. In the parable of the vine and the branches, the theme 'Abide in me and I in you' (John 15.4) occurs repeatedly. It cannot of course be assumed that these are the *ipsissima verba* of our Lord himself; but it is not unreasonable to suppose that the thought constitutes an element in his own teaching transmuted into Johannine idiom. Hence, though direct borrowing by St Paul from the Gospel tradition is not capable of proof, the phrase 'in Christ' may well be representative of an equivalent idea traceable to our Lord himself.[2]

Another consideration imparts weight to this supposition. C. A. A. Scott draws attention[3] to a contrast with the Synoptic Gospels, arising from 'the fact that another preposition (μετά) is there used to describe the companionship of the disciples with Jesus, a preposition which is never employed by St Paul for that purpose'. The preposition is used in the simplest definition which the Gospels offer of the reason for there being an inner Twelve at all: Mark 3.14, 'And he ordained twelve, that they should be with him,' while the Johannine version (John 15.27) is: 'Ye have been with me from the beginning.' It is not difficult to see the reason for this discrepancy. When in the days of the incarnation men were the companions of Jesus, it is natural to speak of them being with him. When St Paul

---

[1] *A Man in Christ*, London 1935, 156.

[2] So Sanday and Headlam, *Romans* (International Critical Commentary), Edinburgh 1900, 161: 'It is natural to ask whether all can be accounted for on the assumption that the phrase originates entirely with St Paul. In spite of the silence of [the Synoptic Gospels] it seems more probable that the suggestion came in some way ultimately from our Lord himself. This would not be the only instance of an idea which caught the attention of but few of the first disciples but was destined afterwards to wider acceptance and expansion.'

[3] C. A. A. Scott, *Christianity according to St Paul*, Cambridge 1939, 152.

uses his characteristic phrase 'in Christ', he is talking of another order of fellowship. Carnal limitations no longer intervene to make simple compresence the only relation possible. A new possibility is opened up by Christ's exalted withdrawal of himself from visible presence with them. This is the 'expediency' which he himself ascribes to his going away from them. That this is the explanation of the use of the two prepositions is corroborated by three further facts. St Paul never uses the expression 'in Jesus Christ' but, when the two names are conjoined, always and only 'in Christ Jesus', and we have to wait till post-apostolic times for this apparently deliberate distinction to be blurred.[1] The second piece of evidence is found in the use of the phrase 'in me' in the Fourth Gospel. As the High Priestly Prayer is offered, it is as much the exalted Christ as the incarnate Jesus that is presented; the line of distinction between them has almost disappeared. But more: there is a further stage and level of experience in which the Johannine and the Pauline conceptions, different as they characteristically are, meet. It is at the end of time. For of this stage both traditions unite to use the phrase 'with Christ': John 17.24, 'Father, I will that they also, whom thou hast given me, be with me where I am; that they may behold my glory'; and Col. 3.3, the Christian's life is 'hid with Christ in God'. 'Note,' says C. H. Dodd,[2] 'that Paul constantly uses *with Christ* of the future status of Christians, as distinct from their present state *in Christ*.' Thus, when the difference of orientation is taken into account, there is a striking similarity and congruity between the language of St Paul and certain elements to be found in the Gospels.

Later reference will be made to these facts. In the meantime, comparison of the Pauline 'in Christ' with possibly equivalent expressions elsewhere in the New Testament, and examination of the allied expression 'with Christ' in St Paul and the rest of the New Testament, lead to the same conclusion. However novel the use made by St Paul of the phrase 'in Christ', and however unprecedented the emphasis which it acquires in his theology, the idea itself is not a pure invention. There is elsewhere in the New

---

[1] Two remarks may be made about the use of the formula in the sub-apostolic age: first, that it plays a small part and occurs comparatively infrequently; and secondly, that while in Clement of Rome the phrase 'in Christ' appears oftener than any other variant, in Ignatius 'in Jesus Christ' virtually replaces the Pauline 'in Christ Jesus'. See both Deissmann, op. cit., and W. Schmauch, Ἐν Χριστῷ, Gütersloh 1935. The latter concludes (178 ff.) that 'the formula cannot be construed any longer as articulated to the variant meanings on which the sense of the Pauline formula is based'.

[2] *Romans* (Moffatt New Testament Commentary), London 1932, 89.

Testament an element of dominical origin upon which St Paul has seized. He discovers this element to be a fit expression for his own deepest religious experience and understanding;[1] he makes of it a cardinal concept in his theology; he expands and amplifies it with remarkable and rewarding fertility; and he endows it with a prominence and importance which merit attention.

3. The meaning of the phrase

The more important though not unrelated question of the meaning of the phrase has now to be faced. In the case of Christian readers of the New Testament who have seen and used the two words so often, familiarity tends to breed, not perhaps contempt, but certainly disregard. We tend to forget that there is no other proper name that could intelligibly stand after and governed by the word 'in'. As J. S. Stewart says,[2] 'We do not speak of being *in* St Francis, or *in* John Wesley.' Nor is this simply a peculiarity of the English language or of the day in which we live. In Greek literature, ἐν is found governing a personal singular, but, as Deissmann reminds us,[3] it is a very rare usage. If, as has been suggested, the phrase has approximate equivalents in the words of Jesus himself, they must have struck his hearers as unusual and surprising. Indeed it may have been their perplexing character which prevented their easy or frequent assimilation into the Christian *kerygma*, until their latent significance was realized by the awakened sensibility and apprehension of St Paul.

Deissmann's monograph initiated serious consideration of the phrase and pioneered a new understanding of Pauline theology. Accordingly it is right to begin the discussion of the meaning of the phrase with what he says. After an exhaustive examination, he draws the following conclusion:[4] 'St Paul constructs the formula ἐν Χριστῷ ᾽Ιησοῦ out of a usage already present in secular speech. The phrase characterises the relation of the Christian with Jesus Christ as an existence in the pneumatic Christ locally conceived. For this thought there is no analogy in any other relation of man with man. But we may clarify it by the analogy of the concept underlying the expressions ἐν πνεύματι and ἐν τῷ Θεῷ, the concept of dwelling

---

[1] See J. Weiss, *The History of Primitive Christianity*, 465 ff. Weiss allows the question of the historical origin of the phrase 'in Christ' to merge into this 'psychological problem', and here it is finally submerged.

[2] *A Man in Christ*, 154.   [3] *Die nt Formel*, 70.   [4] Ibid. 17 f.

in a pneuma-element comparable with air. The question whether the idea of locality which is the basis of the formula is to be understood in its proper sense or merely as a rhetorical metaphor cannot be certainly decided; but the first possibility has the higher degree of probability. In any case, whether understood literally or metaphorically, the formula is the characteristic Pauline expression for the most profound fellowship conceivable between the Christian and the living Christ.' This statement is amplified in a later work[1] as follows: 'This formula—so closely related in meaning with the phrase "in the Spirit"—must be conceived as the peculiarly Pauline expression of the most intimate possible fellowship of the Christian with the living spiritual Christ. . . . Just as the air of life, which we breathe, is "in" us and fills us, and yet we at the same time live in this air and breathe it, so it is also with the Christ-intimacy of the Apostle Paul: Christ in him, he in Christ.'

At least three points here are notable. Deissmann holds that in St Paul's thought there is a close connection between Christ and the Spirit. In the later work, the qualification 'spiritual' is added to the attributes accorded in the earlier to the Christ with whom the Christian has fellowship; and this may indicate an increasing emphasis in Deissmann's thought upon the spiritual character of the relation. Further the relation of the Christian with Christ as thus conceived is evidently thought of as mystical; and it may be asked whether mysticism can, in any ordinary sense of the term, be applied to St Paul's thought. Both these points will be better considered a little later. In the meantime, there is the third notable point, the 'local' significance which Deissmann attributes to St Paul's use of 'in Christ' and Deissmann's preference for a literal rather than a metaphorical understanding of it. Since the Christ with whom the Christian has this fellowship is to be spiritually understood, and consequently the relation is interpreted mystically, it is a little difficult to understand this preference. But there is a greater difficulty. If the local significance of the phrase be pressed, the Christian must be conceived as being brought into the proximity of the exalted (and spiritual) Christ, for no other Christ may be said to be local now. The question then arises how the Christian is related to the work which was accomplished not by the exalted Christ but by the incarnate Christ. It would be a grave impoverishment to think of this work as merely a means for bringing the

[1] *Paul*, 140.

B

Christian into contact with a spiritual Christ. Yet, if stress be laid upon the local significance of the phrase, it is hard to see what more that work accomplishes.

Deissmann's monograph occasioned immediate and widespread interest. It was generally recognized that an important issue had been raised, even if the conclusions reached did not command complete assent. Perhaps the most general criticism was that Deissmann pressed a unity of meaning too rigidly upon the phrase. So Weiss wrote:[1] 'It is, it seems to me, a mistake of Deissmann . . . when he assumes that in all passages the phrase carries the same emphasis.' The variety evident in St Paul, which in some degree Deissmann does in fact recognize, is ignored when 'Christ-mysticism is represented as the prevailing, characteristic mark of Pauline religion'. In the long analytical note referred to above, Weiss lists several meanings of the phrase different from each other and from the mystical sense which Deissmann emphasizes. Further, Weiss observes that 'the formula also occurs frequently simply as an expression denoting to be a Christian'. The importance of this simple use does not appear to have been realized by Weiss; but the analysis he makes establishes the fact that the use to which St Paul puts the phrase is various and not uniform.

4. *Christ and the Spirit*

The accounts given by Deissmann and Weiss elicit two matters about which it is necessary to come to some conclusion. The first concerns St Paul's conception of the relation between Christ and the Spirit. At this point, Deissmann and Weiss agree that St Paul virtually identifies the two. Deissmann points out[2] that the Pauline 'Christ in me' is a 'confession poured forth from the depths of the soul, the confession of an assurance which illuminates and holds under its sway the remotest recesses of the ego'. But corresponding to this confession there is the other expression which is just as characteristically Pauline, 'I in Christ'. Deissmann brings the two expressions together, and comes to the conclusion that 'Christ is the Spirit; therefore he can live in Paul and Paul in him'. This in turn enables him to regard the primary meaning of the formula in St Paul as mystical. 'The Spirit,' he says,[3] 'has nothing of the fleshly, nothing of the earthly; it is divine, heavenly, eternal, holy,

[1] *The History of Primitive Christianity*, 468 n. 22.   [2] *Paul*, 140.   [3] Op. cit. 143.

living and life-giving—these all are predicates which Paul applies to it or could apply, and they can also be applied to the spiritual Christ.'

Weiss comes to a similar conclusion by a road that is only a little different.[1] Starting with the same double phrase, that an individual is 'in Christ' and 'Christ is in him', he argues that the conceptions here can only be understood by means of the parallel modes of expression used, e.g., in Rom. 8.9 f.: 'ye are in the Spirit', 'the Spirit of God dwells in you', 'if any man have not the Spirit of Christ'. 'What is true of Christ is true also of the Spirit, and the reverse.' 'Fundamentally, the reason for this representation lies in the fact that Christ and the Spirit are in some way identical'; and II Cor. 3.17 is cited: 'The Lord is that Spirit.' 'This manner of thought is possible only upon the supposition that—at least at the moment when the formula was first conceived and expressed—the fixed outlines of the personality had been softened and dissolved, and replaced by the idea of a formless, impersonal, all-penetrating being.'[2]

The real difficulty which such an emphatic view faces is evident. On any showing, the encounter of the unconverted Saul on the Damascus road with the risen Christ is determinative. The account of this event appears three times in Acts, and on two occasions the narrator is St Paul himself. In two cases, he with whom the encounter takes place is named 'Jesus', and in the third 'Jesus of Nazareth'. In his own letters, St Paul refers at least once to the incident, when in I Cor. 15.8 he declares that Christ 'was seen of me also', and he thereby classifies himself with those others, the twelve and the brethren, who had seen the risen Lord. Is it really probable that the apparently personal impression made upon St Paul at this decisive moment could ever be supplanted by the formless and impersonal conception which Weiss attributes to him? And if it did so, how then shall we account for the recurrence of such a distinction as is involved in II Cor. 3.15, where the concluding benediction is given trinitarian formulation?

Deissmann states the almost certainly necessary qualification at this point.[3] It may be a 'spiritual Christ' that St Paul has in mind when using the formula; but at least this 'Spirit-Christ' is 'no feeble, indistinct image set up by the phantasy-producing power of

---

[1] *The History of Primitive Christianity*, 464.
[2] Ibid. 465.　　　　[3] *Paul*, 143.

religious imagination, which evaporates into a boundless, empty cloudland; on the contrary, he has his hold on concrete reality at the cross. He is, and remains, the crucified.' Deissmann does not, however, make it very clear how the Spirit-Christ can be conceived as retaining this firm hold upon the concrete historicity of the cross, and it is doubtful whether the two ideas can really be made congruous. But the statement at least imposes limits upon the closeness with which Christ and the Spirit are to be identified: it may still be possible to say 'Christ is the Spirit'; but clearly some reservation is implicit, for no one will wish to affirm that 'the crucified' is Spirit. There remains a difficulty here that has not been solved. If the Christ St Paul means when he uses the formula is spiritualized, it is certainly easier to reconcile and understand his use of 'I in Christ' and 'Christ in me'; but this seems to imply a disregard by St Paul of the historical and personal aspects of Christ which appear so deeply embedded in his conversion experience, and to suppose such a disregard is too high a price to pay for this way of solving the difficulty. If this is so, Weiss does not provide an acceptable solution. On the other hand, it is not easy to represent a 'Spirit-Christ' as holding on to the concrete reality of the cross; and if this is true, Deissmann also falters in the interpretation he offers.

The fault of both Deissmann and Weiss consists in failure to take quite seriously the *assumptio carnis*. They did not fully appreciate the thought lying behind the Chalcedonian concept of hypostatic union—they lived in an age in which appreciation of its importance was not universal. An identification of Christ and the Spirit made it possible to find a meaning in the 'in Christ'. But the solution is too facile, and it is not enough to think of our incorporation into Christ in purely spiritual terms.[1] The humanity of Christ has to be seen in the light of the 'in Christ'; and an attempt to do this will be made in the third chapter.

In the meantime, it may be noted that Deissmann attributes the function of linking the 'Spirit-Christ' with the Christ of history to a third factor—to 'mystical communion with the Spirit-Christ'. He thus commits himself even more deeply to the opinion that the formula has to be understood in a mystical sense. This brings us to the second aspect upon which comment is necessary.

[1] Fritz Neugebauer (*In Christus*, eine Untersuchung zum Paulinischen Glaubensverständnis, Göttingen 1961) represents St Paul as holding together what the Spirit does for man and what Christ does for men; and II Cor. 3.17 has to be interpreted in this light. But he rejects the idea that this reduces Christ to a spiritual being (61–64).

5. Christ-mysticism

This second matter concerns the question in what sense St Paul's thought is to be construed as mystical; or, putting the thing in terms more immediately applicable, does the formula 'in Christ' require to be mystically interpreted? The two exponents of St Paul to whom reference has been chiefly made take different sides at this point, Deissmann holding that a mystical understanding gives the key to the understanding of St Paul, Weiss holding that a mystical understanding is inappropriate. Enough has been said already to indicate how sympathetic Deissmann necessarily is to the mystical interpretation. Opposing it, Weiss makes some points that are important and deserve mention. St Paul's thought does not appear to possess a close enough affinity with mysticism ordinarily understood to support the suggestion of a mystical interpretation. (i) Weiss points out[1] that the characteristic mystical expression, *enthusiasmos*, is not only lacking in St Paul, but is incapable of obtaining entrance into his thought. The word is derived from *entheos*, which does not mean one's being in God, but precisely the reverse, God's being in him. While, therefore, phrases similar to this do occur in St Paul's writings, they are offset by the other form of the phrase, added regularly as complement to it; and this destroys the basis of mysticism. (ii) In contrast to the 'revelling in mystical moods, which manifests itself in the piling-up and arrangement of mystical formulae and in playing variations upon them', what we have in St Paul is the simple recurrent phrase 'in Christ', so brief and compact, and so often used in connection with less exalted moments, 'that one must often doubt whether it is filled with a true mystical, ecstatic content of feeling'. (iii) Even more important is the fact that St Paul does not represent his own personality as 'completely fused' with Christ. On the contrary, at those very points where (as Gal. 2.20) mysticism seems most strongly to be in evidence, the expression of it 'is at once interpreted or qualified by a confession entirely in the spirit of the I-and-thou religion: after he says: "I live no more", the qualification immediately follows: "yet I live".' (iv) More generally, Weiss judges that 'there seems to be lacking in his language the real glow and magic of mysticism, and its express and developed terminology.' (v) Fur-

[1] See *The History of Primitive Christianity*, 467 n. 21, 468 ff.

ther, besides these judgments in which difference of opinion is possible, the following fact has to be noted. Let it be allowed that some of what St Paul says is to be interpreted as a Christ-mysticism in which his Christianity is grounded; and let it be allowed that at such points it looks as if Christ had taken the place of God, 'as if God were completely forced into the background'. To balance this impression, St Paul at other points suggests a certain subordination of Christ to God, and hints of a time to come when Christ will render his kingship to God and himself step back, so that God may be all in all. This is a prospect so far removed from mysticism ordinarily conceived as virtually to exclude it from any theology which thinks in such terms.

Other considerations may be added which further differentiate St Paul's use of the 'in Christ' from mysticism. St Paul's thought is not in the least 'aristocratic'. He proffers the relation connoted by the phrase not for a gifted *élite*. Its application is on the contrary universal in scope. Again, there is no hint in what he has to say of egocentric enjoyment. The relationship in Christ precipitates the individual instantly into the fellowship of the Church which is the body of Christ. Nor is the enjoyment of the relationship represented as an already accomplished *fruitio Dei*. On the contrary, the man in Christ is represented as living in a constant and insurmountable tension. Though he is 'in Christ', he is also demonstrably 'in the flesh'. The Christian life is represented as impregnated by a longing, by a consciousness of not-having. And, for relief from this tension in which he lives, the Christian looks not to the present age in which he lives but to that which is to come. The tension is not to be achieved by spiritual or ascetic discipline but to be awaited eschatologically.[1]

In fairness to Deissmann, it ought to be said that upon the mysticism with which he credits St Paul he does put certain limitations, of such a kind and of such importance that, though the name of mysticism may be salvaged, the substance of the thing has almost disappeared. For one thing he recognizes[2] that the paradox

---

[1] Fritz Neugebauer (*In Christus*) interprets the Pauline 'in Christ' in terms of what Christ has done. The participation implied is consequently a participation in what has been done for us and is not mystical at all. On the one hand, Christ is not a merely pneumatic personality, and fellowship with him is not an essential mystical unity (55; cf. the striking objectivity of the phrase in Phil. 3.10); on the other hand, the Christian is not represented in anything like pneumatic terms (125). Cf. the distinction between St Paul's thought and mysticism drawn by M. Dibelius, *Botschaft und Geschichte* II, Tübingen 1956, 111–59.

[2] *Paul*, 154. The further distinctions made appear on 117 f. and 148 ff.

'I—yet not I' modifies profoundly any mysticism that can be attributed to St Paul. To accommodate this modification, he makes a distinction within mysticism on the basis of the different aims which may be adopted by it, and accordingly differentiates what he calls unio-mysticism from communio-mysticism. The names are self-explanatory, and it need hardly be said that it is the latter type that is attributed to St Paul. This distinction is further supported by correlative distinction between different impulses initiating mysticism. For there is an anabatic mysticism, in which man approaches God, a mysticism of striving or performance, which has its characteristic expression in the acting type of cult; and there is on the other hand a katabatic mysticism, in which God approaches man, a mysticism of divine gift or grace, which has its characteristic expression in the re-acting type of cult. Again it need hardly be said that Deissmann regards the Christian faith as belonging to the second type. This is an acute analysis of mysticism. Deissmann contends that the broad and many-sided distinction he makes is crystallized in the German language by the existence of two words, *Mystik* and *Mystizismus*, the former denoting the true religious attitude, while the latter denotes a debased and spurious imitation. Much of the prejudice that the term mysticism tends to arouse in certain quarters would certainly be allayed if the distinction were observed. If it is applied to St Paul, mysticism in a restricted sense might be ascribed to him.

A further comment which Deissmann makes adds precision to this more specific sense in which he attributes mysticism to St Paul. The passage may be quoted at length.[1] 'It is not yet generally recognized that Paul uses the genitive "of Jesus Christ" in a wholly peculiar manner. We have numerous passages in Paul in which the usual rough classification of "subjective genitive" or "objective genitive" is insufficient. . . . In Paul it would be possible to establish the use of a special type of genitive which might be called the "genitive of fellowship" or the "mystical genitive", because it indicates mystical fellowship with Christ. "Of Christ" is here in the main identical with "in Christ".' Deissmann replies to critics of this 'mystical genitive' by charging them with a lack of feeling for language. For the present purpose, however, the important point is that the use is 'wholly peculiar' to St Paul and at the same time virtually identical with the formula 'in Christ'. This is not

[1] *Paul*, 162 ff.

very different from saying that the mysticism to be found in the apostle is 'wholly peculiar' to him; and if this is so, it becomes a matter of words whether his thought is mystical or not. The mysticism now being attributed to him is based upon divine grace and not on human enterprise; it is exercised by way of response and not as a human endeavour; and it is directed to communion of the human and divine and not to any fusion of the two. Mysticism defined in this way does not involve the obliteration of personality either now or hereafter. On the contrary, it is fully personal in character.[1] Nor does it involve the obliteration of time. The conditions time imposes on us are not abrogated. But Christ himself, being beyond the reach of time, is not limited by these conditions, and so we, though still in time, can yet be in him. The eschatological supersession of temporal conditions is never prematurely anticipated in what St Paul has to say.

The contribution Deissmann made to Pauline studies by drawing attention to the significance of the 'in Christ' is of first-class importance. It is, however, severely limited, first by the spiritualizing interpretation in terms of which his Christology is worked out, and secondly by the mystical character given to the consequent relation between Christ and the Christian. The inaugurator of serious consideration of the 'in Christ' has in general been too closely followed at these two points, and, despite the protest of Weiss, the 'in Christ' has too frequently and uncritically been construed as 'mystical' in some often undefined sense.

If due weight is given to what has just been said, we must look for the essential meaning of the Pauline 'in Christ' in a different direction. It is to be found not so much in the individual relation of the 'I' with Christ and the human experience thus involved, but rather in the objective grounds which make this relation conceivable and possible. Not enough attention has been paid to this objective

---

[1] R. G. Smith in the recent new edition of his translation of Martin Buber's *I and Thou* (Edinburgh 1960) says in the Introduction that he must abate his original conception of Buber as a mystic, in order to call him rather, though tentatively, an existentialist. This is a notable and much needed clarification. So long as the kind of thing that Buber says is called mysticism, whatever its origins in Jewish mysticism, terms are being blurred. In classical mysticism the finite individual does not retain the vigour and reality with which Buber invests him. If mysticism thinks of the finite as equivalent in the end to the unreal or at least to the unstable, the provisional, the transient, it is radically opposed by Buber's affirmation of the equal right of finite and infinite to exist. The fact that they belong to different ontological modes, absolute independence and relative independence, does not diminish the reality with which they are constituted in their respective modes.

reference that the phrase 'in Christ' carries. Referring to the distinction between anabatic and katabatic mysticism, Deissmann quotes with approval[1] that 'the one asserts ability to control God, the other to be controlled by God, the one to compel God, the other to be compelled by God.' Then the really central problem concerning the 'in Christ' is clearly the nature of this control or compulsion which is so divinely exercised that the relation described by St Paul in the formula can exist.

6. St Paul's use of 'in Christ'

The attempt must now be made to give a simple classification of at least some of the ways in which the formula 'in Christ' is used by St Paul. The attempt will not compete with the detailed analytical investigation which Deissmann carried out. Its aim will be rather different, for the question to which an answer is sought is whether, for all the learning and skill earlier exemplified, an important element present in the mind of St Paul has not been left out. This element, for want of a better description, will have to be called the objective element.

We revert in the first place to what was said at the beginning of the lecture. The phrase is used to denote Christians. In Rom. 16.7, 'Salute Andronicus and Junia . . . who also were in Christ before me,' St Paul is simply greeting the two persons named, and characterizes them as 'Christians before ever I was'. In Rom. 16.11, another greeting goes to 'the household of Narcissus, which are in the Lord'[2]—that is the Christian family and house of Narcissus. The use of the formula here is little more than indicative—as if St Paul were saying: you know the Andronicus and Junia, you know the Narcissus I mean—the ones who are Christians. However, it is not a merely formal indication, but also a denotation by quality or characteristic, and it thus amounts to a connotation. That is to say, it defines as well as denotes. A Christian is one who is in Christ.

[1] Paul, 150 n. 1.
[2] Fritz Neugebauer (In Christus) draws a distinction between St Paul's use of 'in Christ' and 'in the Lord'. His thesis is that 'in the Lord' is a relational concept, which refers to the individual's relation to the Lord, determines his relationships with others in the present world, and characteristically takes an imperative form (see part IV, 131–47). It is noticeable that of the persons greeted at the end of the Epistle to the Romans, those named up to Rom. 16.10a are in positions of special importance and St Paul designates them as 'in Christ', while those named from Rom. 16.10b onwards are less prominent and St Paul refers to them as 'in the Lord'. However, the Lord is always Jesus Christ, and in the phrase 'in the Lord Jesus Christ' the basic unity underlying the distinction is disclosed.

It need hardly be said that the uses of the word *en* in the New Testament are manifold, and even those in which a personal subject is connected by the preposition to an object are various. The work of classification done by the lexicographers cannot be repeated here; but a simple exemplary classification must be carried out. (i) There is first of all the simple notion of location, as in Acts 2.11, where the disciples are recorded as being 'all with one accord in one place', or as in Acts 5.25, where a messenger announces to the magisterial authorities that 'the men whom ye put in prison are standing in the temple and teaching'. The relationship connoted here is adventitious and transient: it can be terminated or altered at the will of the persons concerned by the simple process of moving elsewhere. (ii) Again there is exemplified the notion of situation, as in Philem. 13, where St Paul mentions that he is 'in the bonds' or fetters which he has incurred as a result of his evangelical activity. The relationship connoted here is extrinsic, imposed upon the person concerned by factors outside his control and alterable, not indeed by his mere volition, but by a change in external circumstances. (iii) There is further the notion of condition, as in II Cor. 11.27 where St Paul declares among other things that he has frequently been 'in hunger and thirst'. The relationship connoted is intrinsic to the person concerned, and, while dependent on external circumstances, is alterable only as a change in these external circumstances has a correlative change in the person himself. In the light of this brief analysis, it is worth while asking whether the 'in Christ' refers to a relationship like any of these three, or whether it must be regarded as a relationship *sui generis* and quite dissimilar. As has been already said, Deissmann judges that the relationship has its closest analogy to the first usage where locality is primarily intended. But it can with much more justification be regarded as having closest analogy with the third usage: the phrase connotes primarily not an adventitious or external circumstance of the persons concerned, but an intrinsic circumstance properly called a condition. Then the characteristic by which these Christian people to whom St Paul refers are designated is to be understood not so much as a locality in which they may be found, or a situation in which they are placed, but rather as a condition or status to which they have been admitted.[1] Only an interpretation of this kind can

---

[1] Fritz Neugebauer (*In Christus*), corroborating the use of ἐν to signify a situation, condition or status, and establishing the remarkable frequency of the usage, also cites II Cor. 11.27, and adds no fewer than 140 other passages.

elucidate the full meaning of such a passage as Gal. 3.13 f. The blessing of Abraham has (*mirabile dictu*) been made available for the Gentiles. How has this come about? St Paul's answer is, quite simply, 'in Christ' (AV: 'through Christ'); and the elements that constitute this ground are designated as our having been redeemed from the curse of the law, because Christ himself became curse for us, and so created a new Israel of faith to which the Abrahamic promise is applicable. Jew and Gentile may thus be 'all the children of God by faith in Christ Jesus' (Gal. 3.26): it is thus that Christians are constituted.

Again the phrase is apparently used to designate or define conduct. This looks as if it were a secondary and derivative use, dependent upon and determined by the use already mentioned: it is the conduct of those who have first been denoted as in Christ. Thus Rom. 16.12: the characteristic feature of Tryphena and Tryphosa is that they 'labour in the Lord'. Once more the unusual character of the phrase has to be noted. We can indeed speak of working in the factory or in the gasworks, or even perhaps in the university; but we should never speak of working in the shop-steward or in the boss or in the Vice-Chancellor. It is of particular interest to contrast their use of the phrase with a more usual form of words that sometimes also occurs in St Paul, the phrase 'of Christ', as in Col. 4.12 of Epaphras, who is called simply a 'servant of Christ'. In the last resort, the intention of the phrase is not fundamentally different; and yet the fact that different phrases are used implies some kind of distinction. While the simple 'of Christ' implies a more or less external relationship or bond between master and servant, the more unusual 'in Christ' must imply a more intrinsic relationship between the two. Again, St Paul exhorts the Philippians to 'stand fast in the Lord' (Phil. 4.1). The phrase which would more naturally spring to mind is 'for the Lord', as in fact the hymn expresses it: 'Stand up, stand up for Jesus'.[1] No doubt again, the difference between the Pauline use of 'in the Lord' and the more usual 'for the Lord' is not very great. But the fact that St Paul prefers to use his own characteristic phrase indicates that he has in mind, not the external

---

[1] It is recorded that the evangelist C. T. Studd, calling upon his audience at a great evangelistic meeting to do something to symbolize their adherence to Christ, proposed that they should obey the injunction of this hymn, but observed that they were already standing; and accordingly he bade them 'Stand on your chairs for Jesus!' But, even when more was as it were demanded by him, it was still in the formula 'for Jesus' that the demand was made.

relationship which 'for Jesus' suggests, but a more intimate connection, indicative less of an attitude than of a status. Hence the
conduct of those that are 'in Christ' is itself qualifiable by the
same phrase.

A third use of the phrase may properly be distinguished. The
formula 'in Christ' is applicable to the relations of those that are
'in Christ' with others. As determining relations with others,
Rom. 16.8 is an example: St Paul sends greeting to 'Amplias my
beloved in the Lord'. Similarly in Rom. 16.22, he salutes his corre-
spondents not merely as his dear friends, but adds: 'in the Lord'.
And again in Philem. 23, Epaphras is denominated as his 'fellow-
prisoner'; but the community referred to has its ground not in a
mere similarity of situation or circumstance, but 'in the Lord'.
As we may put it, the relationship is based upon a concrete *tertium
quid* in which the two parties participate, namely the common
status which they enjoy and which is described as 'in the Lord'.
With this the close parallel of Col. 4.7 may be compared: the
fellowship of service in which St Paul and Tychichus participate
has its basis 'in the Lord'; and this evidently adds something to
that fellowship.

The formula is applied also to the relationship existing between
members of the Church. The Thessalonians are gathered together
into a church, but the church into which they are thus gathered
'is in God the Father and in the Lord Jesus Christ' (I Thess. 1.1).
More expressly, in Gal. 3.28, the unity which characterizes the
Church is a unity in Christ Jesus: 'Ye are all one in Christ Jesus.'
It is evident that the association to which reference is thus variously
made could have been rendered differently. It could have been
represented as a function of a personal liking or attraction, or of a
common participation in a common misfortune. And the unity
could have been rendered as that of a social entity. The work upon
which St Paul and other Christians are engaged could have been
expressed as a joint loyalty exercised in a common cause. But
St Paul avoids all these associative relations, and deliberately refers
the bond of unity concerned to something theologically more profound. The key to its proper understanding, he declares, is not to
be found in any trivial associative bond, but rather in the 'in Christ'.[1]

[1] This corporate aspect of the 'in Christ' receives treatment at greater length in
Ch. 4, Sect. 10.

7. *The objective meaning of 'in Christ'*

This analysis of St Paul's language makes it clear that his use of the formula embraces virtually the whole range of the life of the Christian. What is connoted by the formula proves to be the determination of a man's being a Christian at all, of his individual conduct, and of his relations with others. This variety of application has proved puzzling to those who have taken the trouble to review it: the question whether there is any distinctive basic meaning to be assigned to the phrase has proved difficult to answer, and the replies given to it have varied. Deissmann exemplifies one kind of reply. Among St Paul's uses of the phrase, he discerned what he calls a mystical use, and this he regards as normative. But this suggestion, though it represents a valuable insight, may be judged not to have survived the criticism so powerfully urged against it by Weiss: St Paul does not manifest elsewhere, or even in all the uses to which he puts the phrase, the mystical temperament and attitude of mind. Weiss himself supplies another kind of reply. He is reconciled to accepting a variety of use on the part of St Paul. But among the various uses, he apprehends some kind of order. There are those which embody a fuller meaning, and there are others manifesting a certain debasement of value. On the basis of those cases where the phrase carries with it little more than the meaning of 'Christian', he judges[1] 'either that Paul did not create the formula, but had taken it over; or if he is the creator of it he used it so frequently that in his hands it has become, so to speak, like a coin which has been thinned by handling.' A reply of similar type is offered by, for example, W. Morgan.[2] Of three main formulae recurrent in the Pauline writings, 'in Christ', Christ in the believer, and fellowship with Christ in his death and resurrection, he maintains that 'the first, though by far the most frequent, stands lowest in definiteness and importance'. 'A careful examination of the many relevant passages will show that it is not possible to regard the formula as conveying everywhere a single uniform idea.' 'On the whole one may conclude that the formula "in Christ" commends itself to the Apostle largely on account of its elasticity, and that while now one relationship and now another may be in the foreground, the meaning is in most cases left more or less vague.'

[1] *The History of Primitive Christianity*, 469 note continued from 468.
[2] *The Religion and Theology of Paul*, Edinburgh 1917, 117–19.

Such a conclusion would be profoundly disappointing, and if it had to be accepted would amount almost to a counsel of despair. But do the facts force us to it? That there is 'elasticity' in the Pauline usage, or better said a manifold variety, is incontestable. But that the idea is characterized by 'vagueness' is not the only method of making sense of these facts. On the contrary, it may with equal right be suggested that it is not vagueness which enables the idea to appear in such a variety of uses and applications, but the basic importance which it possesses. On this reading of the facts, it would follow that it is wrong to regard the use of the formula when equivalent simply to 'Christian' as being a debasement of its value. The right interpretation would rather be that, concealed in the formula 'in Christ', is the ultimate basis of being a Christian and of the life that emanates from this.

If this interpretation is followed, the mystic interpretation cannot be regarded as normative. The reason for this is not that the interpretation is necessarily wrong in itself, but that it focuses attention on the nature of the relation connoted by the phrase and disregards the basis on which the relation, whatever its nature, alone rests. It is what the grace of God in Jesus Christ has done that makes the relation a possible and real thing. If the essential reference of the phrase is to this, then it is no wonder that it should occur with such frequency and be employed in so wide a variety of applications. God has laid the foundation for a new humanity and a new life: it is to this mighty work that the phrase 'in Christ' testifies.

That this interpretation of the Pauline 'in Christ' is both possible and likely has been affirmed by Fritz Neugebauer in the most recent considerable study of the formula.[1] The author argues that the most important concept in Pauline anthropology is that *person* is to be understood in terms of 'what it does and what happens to it' (*was sie tut und was mit ihr geschieht*, 53). St Paul interprets Christ in the light of this same anthropological concept. His person and his work must be understood together: *Christum cognoscere hoc est: beneficia eius cognoscere, non eius naturas, modos incarnationis intueri* (54). A careful examination of the constructions with ἐν in the Pauline corpus establishes the striking frequency with which ἐν

---

[1] Fritz Neugebauer, *In Christus*. The book appeared after the argument of the present work had been completed and just before the process of publication began. It constitutes the most detailed study of the formula in recent times, and powerfully emphasizes the objective character of the formula which it is the aim of the present work to present and apply.

denotes '*allgemeine Umstandbestimmungen*' (general determining circumstances), the *Umstände unter denen etwas ist oder geschieht* (38 f.). On these lines the material content of the formal 'in Christ' is definable. Christ represents the circumstances in which St Paul conceives the end of the law (II Cor. 3.7–14), the blessing of the Gentiles (Gal. 3.13) and the confirmation of the promises of God (II Cor. 1.19 f.) (80 ff.). Hence salvation is the deed of God which happens in him whom God has set forth as *hilastērion* (83); and a Christian is simply one who is 'in Christ', who, in other words, is determined by the event of Christ (126).[1]

Here then is further confirmation that an objective interpretation alone rightly represents St Paul's understanding of the phrase. The following chapters will examine the implications that follow when this is taken seriously.

[1] On the basis of II Cor. 5.17 and Phil. 4.21, Neugebauer thinks such a definition is directly applicable to all Christians, even if at times St Paul seems to limit its application to certain individuals specially charged with the proclamation of the Gospel.

2

The Recipient of Life in Christ

1. *Implications of the 'in Christ' for the understanding of man*

EVEN if there is no single meaning with which St Paul invests the phrase 'in Christ', some meanings are more basic than others, and among these is that proper to the phrase in its simplest use, when it defines what a Christian is. In this use it refers to the relation in which a Christian stands to the source from which are derived both the status and the benefits he enjoys. This meaning enables the phrase to be used in the great diversity of applications and with the varying degrees of fulness apparent in St Paul's thought; and to understand it as carrying this meaning as primary is to make sense of facts which have otherwise been found baffling. But it also involves important theological implications, and to the exposition of some of these the rest of what is said will be devoted.

To begin with, the 'in Christ' has implications for the Christian understanding of man. For if it defines the Christian, it follows *a fortiori* that man must so be understood that to be in Christ is a possibility for him. If we were prohibited from saying this, we should have to make up our minds that it is a matter of sheer miracle when a man becomes in Christ and so a Christian. That there is something miraculous here will hardly be doubted by anyone concerned with the Christian faith: of course it is God's own work that it should happen at all. But if it were construed as sheer miracle, we should be acquiescing in the view that between the man before and the man after conversion (or however we designate the dividing line) there was no continuity at all. When therefore we use the term man for the being on both sides of this dividing line, we should be using the word in a purely equivocal sense. This St Paul for example does not encourage us to do. Of men before conversion, St Paul says that they 'hold the truth in unrighteousness' (Rom. 1.18), and they 'reply against God' (9.20)—

but they are men who do this. Of men after conversion, St Paul says: 'if any man be in Christ, he is a new creature' (II Cor. 5.17)— but he is still a man for whom this transforming event occurs. To be in Christ must then be construed as a possibility which neither *ab origine* initiates nor finally ends a man's being a man. Man has therefore to be understood in such a sense that he can be in Christ. This implies not that God has nothing to do with the transition that takes place, but that God's part in the event is of such a kind that there is no absolute break in continuity between the man that was and the man that now is in Christ.

But in saying that man must be understood in such a way as makes the 'in Christ' a possibility for him, we may already be mis-stating the case; or more accurately, we may so be stating it that only one view of how this possibility becomes his is available to us. For to put the matter in this way is at least near to saying that man must be capable of being a Christian; and this in turn is only a short distance away from saying that we must find resident in man certain qualities and capacities in virtue of which this possibility can become his. It is on this basis that Plato has figured from time to time as in some sense a Christian philosopher, and the doctrine of the *anima Christiana naturaliter*[1] has been erected. The strain in Christian theology of which this is representative must later be looked at more closely. But to accept it now would be to give a reply of a specific character to the question concerning man's nature. This reply may indeed be right, but we must not thus early prejudge it to be necessarily so. All that is being said at the moment is that man must be understood as one who has before him the destiny of being in Christ.

2. *The testimony of Genesis*

In recent theology, a serious attempt has been made to discover the biblical view of man and his nature. Nothing has done more to focus attention on this theme and to awaken realization of its importance for determining how we shall answer the question concerning the nature of man than the now famous or notorious contro-versy between Barth and Brunner.[2] The debate was conducted with unfortunate acrimony, but at least the protagonists of the opposing views took with absolute seriousness what the Bible had

---

[1] The phrase is to be found in Tertullian, *Apologeticus* 17.
[2] See *Natural Theology*, London 1946.

to say about man. If it ever was excusable to disregard the biblical view, it is so no longer. Nor is it now possible to regard what is said in the Genesis account of man as merely a piece of picturesque and archaic folk-lore. The reason why we are required to turn to what Genesis has to say need not be found in the supposition that the Bible is divinely inerrant. Many could not hold such a reason as valid. The reason is to be found less precariously in the fact that the New Testament is theologically connected with and arises out of the Old Testament; that Christ himself stands within this stream of thought in which development is no doubt to be discerned; and because those who witness to Christ, and who therefore make use of the 'in Christ', stand similarly within this stream and, so far from breaking with the Old Testament conception, endorse it.

For understanding the meaning of 'in Christ' it is therefore important to reckon with this Old Testament conception. A brief statement of the salient points which the Genesis account makes may therefore be offered.

The first point is so evident that it requires no emphasis: man is a creature of God: 'Let us make man' (Gen. 1.26). Man is therefore to be regarded as unambiguously upon the created side of things—he does not have his being from himself but from God and by God. On the other hand, it is from God and by God that he has it, and this precludes the idea that creation itself has given rise to his existence—it is not in virtue of some cosmic accident or some fortuitous biological mutation that he makes his appearance upon the created scene. Man is of the creation but not from it. His relation to it is suggested by the place his creation occupies in the Genesis narrative, as also by the special commission concerning his dominion over it: he is the crown and the consummation of the divine work of creation.

In referring to God who effects the creation, the writer of Genesis uses the plural: it is 'let us' which introduces this stage. The phrase implies something for the nature of him who is thus engaged: here is a plural of majesty, a solemn mode of speech usually employed with reference to a sovereign. The plural is used in this way elsewhere in the Old Testament. 'Lord' and 'master', even when applied to a single person, may carry a plural form (as Gen. 39.20; Ex. 21.29, 34; Isa. 19.4) to imply dignity;[1] and the usual Hebrew word

---

[1] See commentaries ad loc., e.g. S. R. Driver, *Genesis*[2] (Westminster Commentaries), London 1904.

for God, Elohim, is itself plural, indicative perhaps of plenitude of attributes and powers.[1]

Further, the use of the plural here and only here in the narrative seems to draw deliberate attention to the unique character of this phase in the creation. The dignity accorded to deity marks the solemnity of the occasion.

With the next phrase in the Genesis account, we come to the point which for the purpose here is crucial. The words are 'in our image, after our likeness'. The meaning which they convey is not easily determined. A difference of opinion manifests itself over a preliminary matter. Do the Hebrew words represented by 'image' and 'likeness' carry different meanings? On the one hand, von Rad,[2] for example, thinks that the apparently careful use of different prepositions to govern the two words implies a difference of 'nuance'. On the other hand, S. R. Driver[3] believes that a difference of meaning is untenable: substantially 'both words refer here evidently to spiritual resemblance alone'; and he rejects the differentia between them that 'image' suggests the relation of living model to its reproduction and conveys the idea of a material resemblance, while 'likeness' suggests the correspondence between model and its representation and conveys the idea of immaterial resemblance.

But the fact is that Irenaeus did press a distinction, maintaining that there is a double element in man. The 'image of God' was identified with man's freedom and rationality, and the 'likeness'

---

[1] As is well known, the Fathers read into the plural more than this, and were accustomed to interpret it in terms of a plurality of persons in the Godhead and thus as anticipatory of the doctrine of the Trinity. Calvin accepts this view (*Inst.* 1.13.24; cf. also *Comm.* ad loc.): 'I know that some scorners ridicule our concluding a distinction of person from the words of Moses, where he introduces God thus speaking: "Let us make man in our image." Yet pious readers perceive what a trivial inappropriate thing Moses would have made of this conference, if in the one God there had not subsisted a plurality of persons.' The argument continues: 'Now it is certain that they whom the Father addressed were uncreated; but there is nothing uncreated except the one God himself. Now, therefore, unless they concede that a power to create, and authority to command, were common to the Father, the Son, and the Spirit, it would follow that God did not speak within himself as only this supposition allows, but must hold that God directed his conversation to some external agents.' It is at any rate true that in the New Testament the Son and the Holy Spirit are associated with the Father in the work of creation (see John 1.3; Heb. 1.2). In an earlier day the suggestion of an inchoate reference to the Trinity could be dismissed summarily, with such words as S. R. Driver uses (Commentary ad loc.): 'This is to anticipate a much later stage in the history of revelation.' But today many theologians would hesitate to reject the suggestion so cavalierly.

[2] G. von Rad, *Genesis*, Eng. trs. (Old Testament Library), London 1961, ad loc.

[3] Commentary ad loc.

was equated with that self-determination in accordance with the divine intention in which consisted the *iustitia originalis* as a divine gift of supernatural communion with God, and this is still the view of the Roman Church.[1] The consequences of this early distinction are momentous and, as we shall later see, crucial. But it is difficult to maintain on linguistic grounds. There seems no trace of it in the following verse (Gen. 1.27), nor does it appear at Gen. 9.6 and 5.1, where the single terms occur without apparent difference of connotation; and Luther deemed it necessary to abandon it upon the simple ground of Hebrew linguistic parallelism. Those who are open to conviction by the Hebraists do not seem anxious to emphasize the distinction, and most of them would endorse von Rad's judgment that 'the whole man is created in God's image'.[2] It is certainly false to impose on Hebrew thought, whether here or later, a deliberate distinction between body and soul, between the material and the spiritual, a distinction which is more classical than Semitic. Thus if the distinction is to be employed in defining the nature of man, it will not be possible to cite the Genesis account of man's creation in its support. What is stated there is said of man as such and as whole, not of man already conceived as broken up into discrete or distinct parts.

3. Divergence of interpretation—the relational view

At this point, the ways diverge sharply. Man is made in God's image and after his likeness—what does this tell us about the nature of man ? One interpretation affirms that the biblical statement must be understood in relational terms: its purport is that man was made in and for a certain relation to God and that the key to his nature is to be found in this relation. The other interpretation reads the statement in substantial terms: that man is made in the image of God means that he bears in himself as at least relatively his own that which makes him man. The two interpretations are not necessarily mutually exclusive. It would be difficult to affirm that the essence of man is purely a relation; clearly he has some kind or degree of substantiality, and unless the term relation is being used in an unusual sense it is two correlates that are related by it. On the other hand, when man is regarded in virtue of being made in God's image as substantial, there is no thought of setting him up as some-

[1] See Brunner, *Man in Revolt*, Eng. trs., London 1939, 93. [2] Op. cit. 56.

thing in his own absolute and independent right; clearly no one is going to hold that his substantiality is such that it severs all relation between him and God. The difference here involved is one of emphasis. But it is not merely a difference of degree for it implies a difference in the way in which the relational and the substantial aspects of man are conceived, and this in turn involves a difference in our understanding of man which is quite radical. The difference appears and reappears throughout the theological debate of today. We are dealing not with a nice distinction which in the end is of trivial importance, but with an issue which forces its way into many and perhaps all serious theological discussions. The questions: what must I do to be saved? what is faith? how is the Gospel to be communicated? will be answered differently according to whether one regards man in relational or in substantial terms. The attempt will now be made to characterize each of these views further.

The relational view is developed in terms of personal connection between God and man, and this it is best frankly to call communion or fellowship. It is true that the term image could not alone yield support for such an interpretation. But then image is by itself not a self-interpreting term; it has to be helped out by other contextual data which the Genesis account supplies, and these when assembled point in the relational direction. For one thing, throughout the account God himself is represented as active will, limited apparently by no lack of power to effect what it wills. Thus in five successive stages the things that are are brought into being by the mere fiat of this will: he wills them and they come forthwith into being. Further, as he proceeds to the sixth stage of his action, he is represented as breaking into speech. It is true that speech is recorded of him earlier, and the other stages are marked with the repeated 'let there be'. But this is not speech in the full sense—not conversational speech, not the medium of communication. Before the creation of man, God for the first time uses speech in a fuller sense: 'Let us make man', and thus enters into colloquy with himself. Again it is true that he is not represented as speaking to a genuine other: he deliberates with himself, since there is no other with whom he can, let alone must, take counsel (cf. Isa. 40.13; Job 38.36). Following upon the divine internal colloquy, man is brought into being. Here two things have to be remarked. That which is here and now brought into being is said to be made in the image of God, as already seen; and with that which is here and now brought into being God enters into the speech of address, if not exactly of conversation. No sooner is man made than God addresses him: 'Be fruitful . . . and have dominion . . . behold, I have given you every herb', and so on. The characteristic and unique mark of that which is made in the image of God is matched by a characteristic and unique mark of the dealings of God with this that has been made, namely the speech in which he engages him. It is not explicitly said that there is any connection between the two facts; but the taut and economical nature of the narrative strongly suggests that there is an essential connection between them. On this basis we may therefore suppose that being in the image of God and being addressable by him are not two things but in the last resort one only. In other words, the image of God in man is to be understood as primarily a relation between God and man whom he has created, a relation which is of the order of communion or fellowship. Wilhelm Vischer expresses this view succinctly when he says:[1] 'The eternal I created [man] in his image and placed him *vis-à-vis* himself as the summit of creation, as the Thou. . . . This intention of God is so serious, that man can only really live in this relation of encounter (*cette relation de vis-à-vis*).' Thus, as Jean Cadier says:[2] 'Man is a being of relation. He does not exist by himself in an egoistic isolation. He exists only by God and for God. He has no value in himself; he was not created for his own glory; he exists only to manifest on earth the glory of God.' A similar conclusion is drawn by D. Cairns[3] who says that the Genesis account 'means by existence in God's image a personal responsible existence before God'.

So much can be said about the nature of man presented by the account of his creation in Genesis without going a single step beyond what the data supplied warrant. The fact is that the account given is a purely theological account: the essential nature of man is not conceived anthropologically; it is found in *that* he is by God and *what* he is for God. Of course it is true that all things are in some sense constituted by their relation to God—'By him all things consist' (Col. 1.17, cf. 16). But man's being is constituted by a quite

---

[1] *La Loi*, 67, quoted by Jean Cadier, 'Études bibliques: 1: L'Image de Dieu', *La Revue Reformée* IX 3, 1958, 16.

[2] Ibid. To this article a good deal is owed in what has been and will be said.

[3] David Cairns, *The Image of God in Man*, London 1953, 24. This is a detailed study of the concept in all its aspects, some of which, e.g. the effect of the fall, are not relevant to the present purpose.

specific and unique relation. The uniqueness of the relation is brought out by expressing it in two terms, representing aspects that are complementary. The relation in one aspect is a relation of grace. Properly speaking, grace belongs to God in his dealings with man alone. No doubt it is possible and right to think of God as gracious in his dealings with things other than man. But we could not there come to know that grace was predicable of God, because he can there be called gracious only in a transferred or weakened sense. It is not in Ps. 19 that God is called gracious, but in Ps. 103; and the 'law was given by Moses, but grace and truth came by Jesus Christ' (John 1.17). In its other aspect, the relation must be understood as an interrelation. Linguistics alone might prepare us for this; for if *charis* or grace constitutes God's action, *charis* also, but now equivalent to gratitude, constitutes man's response,[1] and this can be given or withheld. Thus a unique precariousness characterizes man's relationship to God, such as is found in the case of no other thing. When we describe man in these theological relational terms, resisting the temptation to find his essence in some other thing, we stand at the point where the Bible stands and beyond which it does not itself go.

But the purity of the theological account is not always maintained even by those who on the whole stand by the relational view of man's nature. Thus W. Eichrodt writes[2] as follows: 'If we remember the whole manner and fashion in which the Godhead is pictured in Gen. 1, how he appears from the first lines as conscious and powerful will, and continually bears witness to himself through insistent purposive creation, we shall be forced to find man's likeness to God as indicated by the author in his spiritual superiority, which expresses itself not only in his higher rational endowment, but above all in his capacity for self-consciousness and self-determination; in short in those capacities which we are accustomed to regard as typical of personality. . . . The gift to man of the *imago dei* in the formal sense indicated by us implies nothing less than a connection with God through which man, even as a sinner, remains a rational being capable of spiritual fellowship with God. His pre-eminence over all other creatures consists in the fact that as a conscious self he can be reached by God's word, and thereby called to responsibility.' This statement is very similar to those quoted above; but it

[1] See P. S. Watson, *The Concept of Grace*, London 1959, 11.
[2] *Theologie des Alten Testaments* II, Leipzig 1935, 60 f. (Eng. trs. in preparation).

includes certain significant additions. What Genesis has to say about
man could not be better stated than by saying that essentially man
'can be reached by God's word, and thereby called to responsibility'.
But other ideas have been infiltrated: 'higher rational endowment',
'capacity for self-consciousness and self-determination', 'those
capacities which we are accustomed to regard as typical of personality', and so on. How have we become 'accustomed' to subjoin
these other 'capacities'? Since the biblical account has nothing to
say about them, the answer must be that we are being determined
in our thinking from some other source. Here Barth's comment[1]
has some justification: 'We cannot discuss which of [such mixed
explanations] is the true explanation of Gen. 1.26 ff. For it is
obvious that their authors merely found the concept in the text,
and then proceeded to pure invention in accordance with the
requirements of contemporary anthropology.' In other words, the
transition has already been made to anthropology. Alongside of
the biblical account which is purely theological, other interpretative
ideas have been added which have their source elsewhere. The
reasons for thus supplementing the biblical account may be praise-
worthy and the results valuable. But it does go beyond what the
Bible here tells us about man. What is thereby added has to be
scrupulously considered in case what purports to be interpretation
becomes paraphrase, and exegesis becomes a reading into instead
of a reading out of the biblical witness. At this point, the second type
of interpretation is coming into view, and to an outline and consideration of it we now turn.

4. *The substantial interpretation*

The interpretation of which a brief account has just been given
is, in the terms in which it has been presented, of very recent
origin. Some of the terms quoted are immediately recognizable as
part of the philosophical terminology current today, and the whole
tendency they represent may therefore seem to be defenceless
against the criticism of Barth just mentioned. Vischer's 'eternal I'
set over against the created 'thou' is of course immediately identifiable with the ideas which modern theology has learned from
Martin Buber,[2] and the view might therefore appear to be simply
arming itself with weapons of contemporary design. Yet the view is

[1] *Kirchliche Dogmatik* III/1, Zürich 1945, 217; Eng. trs., *Church Dogmatics* III/1,
Edinburgh 1958, 193.   [2] See *I and Thou*.

not quite so vulnerable as this, for it has to be remembered that Buber himself is confessedly a learner in the school of the Old Testament. The relational interpretation, even if it is expressed in novel terms, does stay closely to the Old Testament witness.

But besides the relational view, there is what has already been called the substantial view, a view which has in fact for very much longer influenced and even dominated Christian thinking about man, and which is quite opposed to the relational view. The point at which the two views diverge has already been mentioned. When the strictly theological interest and plan proposed in Genesis and in the Bible generally is displaced by an anthropological interest and plan, the character of the exposition instantly alters. The attempt is then made to discover in man something that can be identified either as the image of God itself or as the correlate in man of that image in which he was made. This is to embark on an anthropological analysis of man and, however carefully the analysis is conducted, the primary simplicity of the biblical account of man is on the one hand sacrificed and on the other supplemented from elsewhere. This strand is persistent in Christian theology.

It may be held to begin with Irenaeus. As already said, he forces apart the 'image' and the 'likeness' of Genesis 1, and allots to them different and distinct connotations. The second he regards as divine gift and identifies it with supernatural communion with God; the first he locates firmly in man's own nature and identifies it with the *humanum*, that which makes man man. What may seem a slight distinction reveals its importance in face of the acid test of sin: with the fall, the second is altogether lost, but the first is retained intact. Irenaeus thus initiates the long discussion which has continued throughout the course of Christian theology. It has been recently revived in the controversy of Barth and Brunner, in which an attempt was made to answer the question: what happens to the *imago dei* under the impact of sin? To some extent, the interest of Christian theology has thereby been diverted. Certainly the question is of the utmost importance. What has, however, not been so clearly seen is that the terms in which Irenaeus posed the question determines not indeed the answer directly, as though only one were possible, but the kind of answer that can be given. The underlying assumption is that the *imago dei*, or some part of it, is a quality or faculty resident in man himself. If this assumption is accepted, we have already aligned ourselves with the tradition which regards the nature of man as substantial rather than relational. When the relation between God and man comes to be thought out (as of course does happen, for the substantial view does not exclude all idea of relation), it has to be conceived as a relation formed between God and that which substantially exists outside him and with which he has in some sense to come to terms. In this schematology, the matter of relation is regarded as of secondary importance. The concept of the *imago dei* still has a part to play, but its reckless identification with one or other of men's characteristics allows attention to be diverted to or occupied by man's nature as such. The biblical conception is evacuated and may then be filled in by considerations that arise from other sources. There is not much doubt what other sources are then employed. The biblical conception of man is supplemented by the contribution of Greek philosophy.

St Augustine provides an apt illustration of this course of thought. Pursuing an anthropological inquiry, he finds three elements in the constitution of man which he calls memory, intelligence and love. These three elements are not accidentally three. They reduplicate in man the trinitarian character of God and represent parallels to the three persons in the Trinity. In terms of what has been said, these three elements form the substantial basis for one end of the relation between God and man. Of course no one did more than St Augustine to emphasize the grace of God. But a tension, in the end unresolved, exists in his thought between the grace of God and that in man with which this grace has to reckon and deal. The third element St Augustine conceives as the complement on man's side to the grace that approaches him from God's side. 'Just as there is no one who does not desire to be, so there is no one who does not desire to be blessed. For how can he be blessed, if he is nothing?'[1] But another rhetorical question may be put: how if he is nothing can he desire to be blessed? and to this St Augustine would give an equally confident denial. Basic for his understanding of man and his consequent relation with God is the thought that man has substantial being. The course of his argument is then plain: because man is, he reaches out to God. But here evidently the wheel has gone full cycle: this order of things is almost the exact opposite of what appears in the Bible. St Augustine says: man is and hence reaches out to God; the Bible says: man is made for God and therefore is. 'The certainty of the *beatum esse velle*,' says Max

[1] *De Civ. Dei* 11.26.

Zepf,[1] 'has as its presupposition self-consciousness, the factuality of the *esse*.' The being of man has been broken off from God, and the mending of the breach is ultimately based upon an element in his own constitution. It is thus that in St Augustine's teaching the desire and search for the *vita beata* gains such prominence. If we inquire how this element has infiltrated into a theology which one might have supposed to have been designed to repudiate it, the answer is to be found in his own words. As Zepf goes on to say: 'Even when in his later years he realises that the realisation of this striving must be awaited from beyond, he himself realizes that in this longing for salvation he is at one with the heathen philosophers.' Thus St Augustine says: 'All philosophers unanimously try to apprehend the life of blessedness, and this is the common ground of their philosophising; but I think also that the philosophers are here at one with us. For if I ask you why you have come to believe in Christ, why you have become Christian, every man will truly answer me: because of the life of blessedness . . . for to seek the life of blessedness, to wish it, desire, long for and pursue it, is I believe what all men do.'[2]

Gilson acknowledges the formula that underlies the thought here. It is that 'all men desire happiness'.[3] But he adds:[4] 'This Greek phrase receives in Augustinianism a new sense. This natural desire for beatitude is an instinct resident in man which God confers upon him, in order to draw him to himself.' But this new sense does not effectively convert the Greek phrase to biblical use. The primary distinction between the substantial and the relational view of man is not thus resolved. Of course God confers gifts upon man. But in what manner are they conferred? On the one view, man preserves a native desire conferred on him by God which is the basis upon which relation to God is constituted. It is a *virtus Dei in creaturas transiens*. God extrudes something from himself and grants it in man an independent existence. On the other, God's gifts are like manna: they can be gathered but not kept. God is indeed at work upon and in man. But this is not to be forthwith construed as a property of man.[5] It is to be suspected that St Augustine's phrase

---

[1] Max Zepf, 'Augustinus und das philosophische Selbstbewusstsein der Antike', *Zeitschrift für Religion und Geistesgeschichte* XI 2, 1959, 106 f.

[2] *Serm.* 150.3.4, Migne 38.809.

[3] Gilson, *Introduction à l'Étude de St Augustin*, Paris 1931, 1 ff.   [4] Op. cit. 139 ff.

[5] See Karl Barth, *Kirchliche Dogmatik* III/3 124 (Eng. trs. 110). Barth declares: 'There can be no question of transferring this honour to the creature' (op. cit. 127, Eng. trs. 112).

remains stubbornly Greek rather than biblical, despite the new sense Gilson tells us it receives, and, if the analysis given of the Genesis passage is correct, it goes beyond what is there said.

Again: *in quibus tria invenit homo, quae diligat: Deum, se ipsum et proximum.*[1] St Augustine invests with trinitarian significance the three forms of love to be found in man. This is indeed a remarkable parallel. Perhaps the best comment upon it is given in the words of Nygren.[2] 'Eros is essentially self-love. To realise this we have only to remember what has been said already about the ego-centric character of Eros. Self-love can be designated as the basic form of all love that springs from Eros. Love of God like love of neighbour, and also all love that has anything other than God as object, can finally be traced back to self-love. Love of neighbour, which seems to have no place within Eros, nevertheless has its sufficient basis there, in that it shows itself as one stage in man's own ascent. And the love of God is based also upon it, since he is the satisfaction of all men's needs and men's longings. On the other hand, Agape excludes all that is meant by self-love. Christianity does not recognise self-love as a legitimate form of love. Christian love has a dual direction, towards God and towards one's neighbour. But self-love appears as the great enemy which must be fought and conquered.' Surely Nygren is right here. But so dominated is St Augustine by a Greek conception of both the power and the seat of love, that he cannot resist crediting man's love of self with the same reality and validity as his love of God possesses.

5. *Calvin's interpretation*

Of the classic theologies perhaps Calvin's treads most delicately between the two types of interpretation. When he refers to the dark side of the picture which the nature of man presents and speaks of the havoc wrought by sin, he freely uses the notion of 'relic': 'some obscure lineaments of that image [of God] are found remaining in us';[3] 'we can trace some remains of the divine image distinguishing the whole human race from other creatures.'[4] The idea is put to good purpose. For it is not only the basis of man's 'inexcusability',[5] but also the ground why men have to be continually reverenced by

---

[1] *De Civ. Dei* 19.14.
[2] See A. Nygren, *Agape and Eros*, Eng. trs., London 1932, I 170; but the quotation here is a translation of the German edition (Geneva, no date), which is clearer at this point.   [3] *Comm. on Gen.* ad 1.26 ff.   [4] *Inst.* 2.2.17.   [5] Ibid. 2.2.18.

other men.[1] Thus presented, Calvin's view seems to endorse the idea that man has something in himself that makes him man and which continues him in being despite the ravages of sin. But the most characteristic expression which Calvin uses to depict the essential nature of man and the meaning of the image in which he was created is 'mirror', and under this concept man's nature appears in quite another light. For this is clearly a relational term, and in fact Calvin works the metaphor out in a relational way. There is, he says, an objective side:[2] 'God looks upon himself, so to speak, and beholds himself in man as in a mirror.'[3] 'Man was therefore created in the image of God, and in him the Creator was pleased to behold as in a mirror his own glory.'[4] But there is also a subjective side; for the mirror actively reflects back God's glory: man 'ought to be accounted a mirror of the divine glory';[5] 'we have to consider how we ought to glorify God in all our life, and hereby see also to what end we are created and why we live. Therefore if we wish to maintain our life before God, we must always aim at this mark: that he be blessed and glorified by us, . . . since he has put his image in us to this end that it should shine forth in us.'[6] We should, he says, 'use our utmost exertions that the glory of God may be displayed by us'.[7] When content is put into the idea of man's glorifying God, Calvin nominates 'true piety, righteousness, purity, and understanding';[8] but the rubric under which all these various excellences are subsumed is that of gratitude: 'it is intended that man should remember whence he received his life in order that he may acknowledge that he lives not by his own power but by the kindness of God alone, and that life is not an intrinsic good, but proceeds from God. . . . He cannot otherwise retain it than by acknowledging that it was received from him.'[9]

Further evidence of this relational view of man in Calvin is to be found in the fact that he represents man's existence as constantly trembling on the verge of annihilation.[10] 'Were it not that God looks

[1] *Comm. on Gen.* 9.5–7, on Ps. 8.5.

[2] The distinction between objective and subjective aspects is worked out at greater length by T. F. Torrance, *Calvin's Doctrine of Man*, London 1949, 35 ff.

[3] *Serm. on Job* 10.7.   [4] *Inst.* 2.12.6.   [5] Ibid. 1.15.4.   [6] *Serm. on Job* 1.6.

[7] *Inst.* 3.6.3.   [8] Ibid. 1.15.4.   [9] *Comm. on Gen.* 2.9.

[10] We should not credit modern thought with originality when it shows itself concerned about the precariousness of man's existence. 'Long before Heidegger, the inspired sages . . . realised to the point of anguish that man is "a-being-made-for-death", that at every instant it is inspired by a power of disintegration, which will make of this living flesh a heap of dust, that its life at every moment escapes it, so freely flows the blood from the wound in its side' (Paul Barrau: *Aux Sources bibliques de l'Existence et de la Vie*, Paris 1959, 9). Cf. Job 30.15.

upon him with a fatherly eye, it is certain that he should be undone
every minute of the hour.'[1] 'As the spiritual life of Adam consisted
in a union to his Maker, so an alienation from him was the death
of his soul.'[2] Yet Calvin does not quite consistently maintain this
view. For in other passages he falls back upon residuary lineaments
of the image, even if these 'are so vitiated and maimed that they
may truly be said to be destroyed'.[3]

6. *The interpretations compared*

The distinction between these two quite different ways of con-
ceiving man's essential nature prompts certain reflections. What has
been termed the relational view preserves some elements of truth
which are obscured or lost in the other. For one thing it emphasizes
with the utmost clarity man's dependence upon God and the correlative fact that only in God does he find his true being. Of course
every Christian account of man admits this and wishes to say it.
But not all accounts find the terms in which it reaches proper
expression. Where man in his essence is declared to be relational,
fit terms have been forged. Jeremiah declares (10.23): 'O Lord, I
know that the way of man is not in himself: it is not in man that
walketh to direct his steps.' To both the truths expressed here the
relational view of man does justice. He can neither be nor rightly
be apart from God who created him. He is made for God, and can
find neither his *esse* nor his *bene esse* outside him.

Again the view elicits a profound truth when it represents the
relation between God and man in terms of the I-Thou of fellowship
and communion. The personalism thereby recognized as charac-
terizing the relation has the fullest warrant from Scripture, whether
we look at Genesis or the prophets or the New Testament. The Old
Testament 'Thus saith the Lord' is balanced by the Word of the
New.

Further, to construe man's nature along the lines proposed by
this view pays proper heed to one of the most notable things about
man: the fact that he, and he alone of all created things, can be and
can also not be. 'To be, or not to be: that is the question'—Hamlet's
famous words, whatever their primary intention, have application
to man in his being. As others have pointed out, common speech
witnesses to this strange and important fact concerning man. One

[1] *Serm. on Job* 5.20 f.   [2] *Inst.* 2.1.5.   [3] *Comm. on Gen.* 1.26–28.

can significantly say to someone: 'Be a man!' whereas one cannot significantly use the words: 'Be a canary!' or 'Be a tiger!'[1]—and this not because animals would not understand but because they cannot be other than themselves or in any way fail to be themselves. Man's being in contrast is characterized by this strange ambiguity that he may be and again may not be a man. To the negative side of man's ambivalent and equivocal nature, the relational view seems to do justice: when his relation to the God who made him is by any means broken, he ceases to be properly man.

But when this has been allowed, it can still be asked whether another aspect of man's nature has not been left out of account. After all, even when the relation to God has been broken, man still in some sense remains man, even if it is a perverted and improper sense. If the nature of man is construed as being purely relational, that is, constituted solely by the relation, it is not easy to accommodate this persistence in being. This is why, as has been said, Calvin frequently resorts to the idea of a residue of the *imago dei* in man, for the metaphor he prefers, that of mirror, serves better to illustrate the positive than the negative aspect of man's nature.

One of the earliest scholarly assessments of Karl Barth's theology was contributed by H. R. Mackintosh in his *Types of Modern Theology*, and one of the criticisms urged there was 'his excessive *actualism*'. By this phrase Mackintosh meant a 'persistent tendency to stress what may be called the dynamic aspects of Christian faith and life at the expense of the static'.[2] The same criticism has been formulated elsewhere[3] under the name of 'eventualism'. The view that man is literally constituted by a relation to God is open to critical comment of this kind. Emphasizing the fact that man does not enjoy his being as an entirely assured possession, the exposition falters when faced with the question of what happens when the relation is broken, when, that is, such negative response is given as destroys it. Can it really be correct to say that 'eternally understood, there are no Christians: there is only the eternal opportunity of becoming Christians'?[4] and is it a right understanding of man that

[1] G. K. Chesterton's familiar variant is in terms of the missionary and the crocodile.
[2] *Types of Modern Theology*, London 1938, 314.
[3] See e.g. W. M. Horton, 'Le Christ, L'Esprit et L'Église', *Revue d'Histoire et de Philosophie religieuses*, 1958, No. 2, 152.
[4] Barth, *The Epistle to the Romans*, Eng. trs., London 1933, 321. So too with reference to service: we may not say that the creature is God's servant or tool or instrument; for the creature may not anticipate its Creator, and so can do nothing but wait to be thus used (*Kirchliche Dogmatik* III/3 60; Eng. trs. 52); and with reference to dogma:

represents his whole being as consisting in nothing but a relation to his Creator? Here there appears to be a defect which has in some way to be remedied.

The alternative view of the nature of man finds its strength where the other is weak. The nature of man is constituted by something less precarious than a mere relation; it is something in its own right, even if when carefully defined it is represented as a divinely conceded right. There is then no question of man's existence terminating when connection with the Creator is fractured, just as all reflection ceases when there is nothing to reflect. The independent existence of man is strongly affirmed—but so strongly, that another question arises. We need no longer be bothered with what happens to man's existence upon the disruption of the proper relation between him and God; but we must be most seriously concerned with what has to be done by man for its resumption. Man's being is not now in doubt: he is regarded as a centre of activity secure in its own existence. Thus the attention is diverted from what man is to what man must do. St Augustine, for example, knows very well that man is quite dependent on the grace of God for both existence and salvation. Yet the way in which he represents grace regularly assumes that God has to deal with him as a substantial centre of activity. The most characteristic way in which he describes the operation of grace is under the rubric of 'infallible attraction'. (We shall have in a moment to note his alternative representation in terms of overmastering compulsion.) God, he says, 'gently leads the elect to desire and pursue goodness by presenting the idea of virtue to them under the most beautiful and seductive guise, and by revealing himself in some measure, albeit imperfect, of his eternal loveliness and glory.'[1] This is already an acceptance of the substantial view of man in preference to the relational. The question of what man has to do is raised before that of what he is has been answered. As independent centre, he is then equipped with reason, freewill or volition, desire, and all the rest of the qualities regarded as characteristically human. He may be impelled into activity in a certain direction, but not compelled, encouraged, not forced. God elicits action from him as children are attracted to their lessons by

'The establishment of a fixed Christian view, of a lasting picture of the relationship between Creator and creature, would necessarily mean that, in taking today the insight given to him, man hardens himself against receiving a new and better insight tomorrow' (op. cit. 65; Eng. trs. 56).

[1] N. P. Williams, *The Grace of God*, London 1930, 33.

the promise of nuts, and sheep to the right path by the offer of a green bough.[1] As N. P. Williams points out, this is simply a moral and religious transcription of Aristotle's cosmology according to which the ultimate being moves the universe as the object of its love.[2]

Regarded as an attempt to answer the question in what the image consists, this suggests that it must be located in a permanent capacity or in an equipment of faculties to be found in man. That this gives a stable basis for man's being is obvious. But the very stability given to it has implications which are disturbing. Man is regarded as sharing being with God. But, according to the Bible, man does not share being with God; he derives it from him. In the last analysis, the whole work of creation is contingent, in the sense that God would be no less God even if it had never been contrived. This is the ultimate difference between the being which men have and the being which is properly God's. If this is forgotten, when the parts to be played by God and man in the matter of salvation come to be allotted, it appears that God has to treat man as an independent centre of activity.

That this is a correct estimate of an errant strain in the history of theological thought is confirmed by the change that comes over the idea of God's grace. It can summarily be said that the simplicity of Genesis leaves us with a virtual identification of image and grace: it is God's grace that he makes man, admits him to communion and requires the response of reflecting his glory. Calvin's insistence upon the importance of gratitude is linguistically corroborated, for as already said, *charis* evokes *charis*, and the image is realized in grateful service and worship. But when man's being is substantiated into a relatively concrete independent existence, grace also becomes substantiated. N. P. Williams[3] suggests that we have Tertullian to thank for this development; for he can speak of 'the power of the divine grace, which is assuredly mightier than nature'. A double thought is expressed here which goes far to estrange the conception of Tertullian from that of Scripture. For one thing, grace now finds its contrary in nature. This exactly reduplicates the situation already noticed: God has to deal with man in the relative independence ascribed to him. So now with grace and nature; terms have to be arranged between the two: *gratia non tollit naturam sed perficit*,[4] and

---

[1] St Augustine, *In Joann.* 26.5.   [2] Κινεῖ ὡς ἐρώμενον, *Met. Λ*, 7, 1027b.
[3] *The Grace of God*, 16 f., quoting Tertullian, *De Anima* 21.
[4] St Thomas, *ST* I qu. 1, art. 8.

D

so on. But whatever the terms, the plain fact is that grace and nature have withdrawn from one another, each into its own relatively independent centre. But on the biblical view, what is opposed to grace is not nature but works. Works are themselves the product not of anything that simply is, but of something that has set itself up in fancied independence. Then repudiation of *charis* as equivalent to God's favour, and the denial of *charis* as equivalent to grateful service and worship, follow as a matter of course.

The other element which Tertullian's phrase expresses is the fateful identification of grace with power, not carefully enough defined to save it from relapsing into the kind of force which is subpersonal, unethical and even mechanical. St Augustine betrays signs of vacillation as he moves between the idea of grace as persuasive and its representation as compulsive. But in fact on both views man appears as something with whom God has to deal upon the basis of some kind of equality until, either by persuasion or by force, he makes his will to prevail. It looks then as if something had gone wrong here too. To conceive of grace as operating by means of attraction, of compulsion, or of supplementation is to defend the existence of man all too successfully: it has become a centre of self-sufficiency of which there is little trace in the biblical account.

7. *Final assessment in terms of the 'in Christ'*

Thus a marked degree of substantiality has been accorded to man with a frequency that marks out a permanent pathway through the course of Christian theology. Is this just one of the optional ways of regarding man, or is it traceable to a deeper cause? Here reference has again to be made to the ambivalency characteristic of man. He both may and may not be a man, and the first option is realized only where there is a response of obedient acknowledgment of the God who made him. So far there is no question of man substantiating himself in this role: all that can be said is that so long as he lives in obedient and joyous communion with his creator he properly is. But there is the dark possibility which Adam embraced. Then the other option is being chosen, and this is, so far as it goes, a substantiation of man's nature. To opt to be not a man is a kind of hypostatization of man's being in false independence. What the fall does, or for that matter what sin does whenever it occurs, is, if we may so put it, to precipitate a potential centre of resistance to God's will and intention, and round about this there coagulate other elements which tend increasingly to make the initial act of dissidence into an independent reality, brandishing its self-sufficiency in the face of the creator. Man then takes sides with other created things, and by the ties of cupidity and desire he is more and more committed to an independence of existence which the rest of creation properly has but which, for the sake of a yet finer destiny, namely to be friend of God, is denied to him. Instead of reflecting the glory of God, he reflects the glory of the universe and of himself.

Not enough attention has been paid to the fact that the capacity of 'knowing good and evil' is attributed to man subsequently to the fall in the Genesis story. This knowledge is supremely the mark of potential autonomy, whatever else has to be said about it. It is indeed in some sense a reminder of God (Rom. 2.14 f.); but it is no less the rallying-point for the most stubborn resistance of man to God and the most radical repudiation of his dependence upon God (Rom. 2.23). The 'good pagan'[1] is always the most difficult subject for conversion.

The long line of Christian theologians who have represented man in terms of the substantial view are quite well aware of the ruinous consequences of sin and the sinful state into which man has fallen. What has not been so clearly seen is that the degree of substantiality with which his nature is credited is largely due to his fallenness and does not properly belong to the state of innocence in which he was created or to the end for which he was designed. When Irenaeus distinguishes between the image and the likeness of the Genesis account, he is really breaking off a hard core round which resistance can organize itself and from which fallen man can maintain a degree of independence over against the God who created him. There is thus attributed to man essentially what is his only in virtue of the sad accident of sin, by right what is consequent upon his misfortune, and as divine gift what really is his only by his 'first disobedience'.

Is it then possible to state the simple relational view of the nature of man that appears in Genesis and the rest of the Bible in such an amended form as will strengthen it at the points at which it is most vulnerable? Man is made for God and his evocation into being, as well as the end in which he finds his true being, consists in just this. So far the statement is simple enough. But it is the shadow side that

[1] See Rosalind Murray, *The Good Pagan's Failure*, London 1939.

demands attention. The story of the fall is the affirmation that man
—and this means all men and each man—turns in disobedience
away from this career and destiny and thus denies that in which he
has both his beginning and his end. It looks then as if he must
simply go out of existence and cease to be. But he does not in fact
seem to do this. As already said, he may only be man in an improper
sense; but he is none the less still to be called man. How are we on
this view to explain his persistence in being? The substantial view
survives this test better, but it discards the simplicity of the Genesis
account; the relational view retains the Genesis simplicity but finds
it difficult to make anything of the man that persists when the
relation has apparently been disrupted.

Are we to say that man persists in being in virtue of his retention
of some imperishable residue of the image, a 'relic' identifiable
despite indefinitely great distortion? Alternatively, is man's continuance in existence to be thought of in terms of a relation which
ex hypothesi has dropped from the personal plane to the impersonal,
so that now, for all the world like a spirited dog fretting at the end
of a held leash, his nature is only negatively qualifiable as antagonism
to God? In the first case, we should be supposing that man still
retains a quasi-property in virtue of which he may still rightly
though imperfectly be called man; in the other, we must content
ourselves with having resort to the sheer faithfulness of God who
for his part declines to disown the relation with the child whom he
has made.

But there seems to be another way. If man persists in existence,
and continues to be what he is, though in a profoundly improper
manner, shall we not be right in thinking that he does so, not in
virtue of anything in himself, and not in virtue of God alone, but
in virtue of the God-man? It is because God beholds us 'in Christ'
that we retain our hold upon existence, or, better said, are retained
in existence.

3

The Author of the Life

1. *Biblical criticism and the person of Jesus*

NEITHER what has been called the relational nor the substantial representation offers a quite satisfactory account of man's nature. At the end of the last chapter, it was suggested that to regard man as being in Christ is a third possibility. The validity of this suggestion can be tested by asking how we may conceive Jesus Christ as sustaining the role and as doing the work which the 'in Christ' requires.

If the scriptural phrase 'in Christ' throws light on the nature of man, it cannot fail to say something also about Jesus Christ. As J. S. Stewart says:[1] 'The fact is that when we speak of being "in Christ" we are consciously or unconsciously making a confession of faith; we are framing a Christology.' The next stage in the argument must therefore be to elicit what the phrase has to say at this point. How must we construe the person of Jesus Christ so that he is able to function as the one in whom man can be said to be?

For about three-quarters of a century,[2] the understanding of the Bible has for many Christians been dominated by the emergence and practice of biblical criticism. The way in which we interpret the Bible has profoundly altered during this time. There were phases when the negative results seemed to be predominant, and simple faith seemed to be endangered. But it is already clear—for biblical criticism still goes on—that there have been immense gains. The new scholarly methods followed have released new light in which the message of the Bible stands more securely and more

---

[1] *A Man in Christ*, 154.
[2] Perhaps eighty years. The term 'higher or historical criticism' appears to have been first used by W. Robertson Smith, *The Old Testament in the Jewish Church*, published in 1881, though Wellhausen was ten years earlier studying Samuel and other parts of the Old Testament on the lines, already foreshadowed by E. Reuss, which were later to be associated with his name.

clearly than before—so much so that the Roman Church, which for long enough was disinclined to accept concepts and results which it represented as the product of unbelief, has more recently adopted a much more favourable attitude.[1]

But biblical criticism has not only affected the way in which we read and understand the Bible; it has profoundly influenced the way in which Jesus Christ has been interpreted. Two distinguishable factors may be said to have operated here, the first arising from the fact of biblical criticism, and the second indirectly from its consequences. Before the advent of biblical criticism, critical methods had of course been applied to secular literary documents; but a certain tact drew a line of distinction between the secular and the sacred. Then almost suddenly, during the third quarter of the nineteenth century, the barrier this distinction interposed between Scripture and the critic gave way, and criticism turned an unimpeded attention upon the Bible. One could now 'interpret the Scriptures "like any other book" '.[2] The almost necessary corollary of this was that the characters appearing in the Bible could be construed and interpreted like any other characters. Must we not then understand the figure of Jesus Christ like any other historical character?

It was true that the biblical record sometimes represented Jesus Christ as very different from any other historical character. If then the witness of Scripture as a whole were taken into account, the effect of the impact of literary criticism might be diminished or even neutralized. But in fact biblical criticism itself removed this sobering influence. For the work of criticism in its early stages undermined the unity of the Bible. There was no 'Scripture as a whole': instead of a unity, there had now to be distinguished several strands, and from the composition thus constituted layers of different character and from different ages could be successively peeled off. The Bible then not only could be studied piecemeal, but must be so studied, if its true character was to be understood. When the unity is thus broken up, and different and not wholly congruent voices made themselves heard, the reader had almost necessarily to think that a choice had to be made between the fragments there collected. He was given a kind of right to pick and choose and to

---

[1] See the papal encyclical *Divino Afflante Spiritu* (1943), and the views that come to frequent expression in *A Catholic Commentary on Holy Scripture* (Edinburgh 1951).
[2] W. Sanday, *Inspiration*, London 1893, 1.

judge some parts as worthier of attention than others. Applying this to the person of Jesus as presented in the New Testament, we are encouraged to believe that he is given to us more reliably in some parts of the record and less reliably in others. From the attitude determined by these two factors, momentous consequences could be expected to flow which would be not only literary but also christological in character.

This was the situation in which there could be and was formulated the question of the historical existence of Jesus. The question was not being raised for the first time; but it was for the first time being asked seriously by those who were not professed unbelievers. Thus Bruno Bauer[1] propounded the provisional hypothesis that Jesus *might* have existed, and gradually worked to the affirmation that the figure of Jesus was in fact no more than the product of Mark's imagination. Similarly D. F. Strauss[2] held that Jesus is a myth; but he did not consider Christianity therefore false: the infinite spirit, he said, is true but not real, the finite spirit real but not true, while the true and the real come together in the identity of man and God in the God-man. The man in this identity is properly the human race as such; but for the simple-minded, it was helpful to represent in a mythical idea what philosophy knew as abstract idea. Such reflections as these are unthinkable apart from the doubt about the authenticity of the Bible which criticism had engendered.

In fact, the idea that Jesus never existed at all was soon discredited. It can now be safely said that, according to the canons of history, no figure has a better claim to historical existence than Jesus. Thus Bultmann can say summarily:[3] 'Of course the doubt whether Jesus really existed is unfounded and not worth refutation. No sane person can doubt that Jesus stands as founder behind the historical movement whose first distinct stage is represented by the oldest Palestinian community.'

But something more has here happened than the mere answering of an important question awkwardly raised. If an affirmative answer is given to the question of the historical *existence* of Jesus, what is being really affirmed is the *historical* existence of Jesus; the denial of the supposition that Jesus is not a historical person endorses the view that he is a historical person. Thus the 'Jesus of history' comes

[1] 1809-92.   [2] 1808-74.
[3] *Jesus and the Word*, London 1935 (Eng. trs. of *Jesus*, Berlin 1934), 13.

upon the scene, and occupies there a commanding place for something like half a century.[1] It was a figure in whose construction
special attention was paid to certain elements in the New Testament
records, while others remained disregarded; and it was a method of
treatment which the critical disruption of the unity of the Bible
had seemed to legitimize. It was a figure rendered as vivid and
accurate as the comparatively meagre data allowed,[2] a two-dimen-
sional figure in terms of length and breadth, and, if the third
dimension of depth was not explicitly denied, little reference was
made and little heed paid to it.[3]

That in this there was immense gain cannot be doubted. 'About
half a century ago a distinguished British theologian spoke of the
recovery of the historical Christ as the most distinctive and determinative element in modern theology, and went on to speak of the
rejuvenescence of theology which was the result.'[4] 'It may safely
be said that practically all schools of theology today take the full
humanity of our Lord more seriously than has ever been done before
by Christian theologians.'[5] In theological terms, Docetism constitutes
a temptation no longer, and it has become generally accepted that
Jesus must be represented as consubstantial with ourselves. We may
put it in more practical terms. A false understanding of the fact that
holiness strictly means apartness can easily invest the sacred with
a non-earthly spirituality which is really indistinguishable from
unreality. The apartness may serve as excuse for exempting what is
shut up there from hard and realistic questioning; and again this
may be at bottom the consequence of doubt whether what has been
thus taken into protective custody can really stand up to such

[1] An American bibliography names over 350 books about Jesus in the English
language alone between 1910 and 1953—see Ethelbert Stauffer, *Jesus and His Story*,
Eng. trs., London 1960, 8.
[2] But cf. *per contra* Stauffer, op. cit., who thinks the meagreness has been exaggerated;
his book represents a fresh attempt 'to give a *historical* account of the story of Jesus' (7).
[3] How recent is the emergence of this interest in historicity can be illustrated by the
way in which the 'holy places' of the Christian faith have been venerated throughout
the Christian era, for example the places where Jesus was born and where he died.
The modern visitor from the West usually visits them with the assumption that veneration will have preserved such places as nearly as possible in the form they possessed
at the date of the historical events with which they are connected. He is astounded and
often offended to discover that no attempt has been made to retain the outward form
in this way, and that imposing ecclesiastical edifices now cover the sites and their
original appearance is quite altered. The fact is that veneration in this form has been
deemed proper for some fifteen centuries of Christian history, veneration of the historical variety for less than one.
[4] D. M. Baillie, *God Was in Christ*, London 1948, 9.
[5] Ibid. 11. But the rise of Demythologizing (see below) subsequent to 1948 might
require a statement not quite so confident.

interrogation.[1] Biblical criticism has at least dissipated this air of unreality; its realistic inquiries pierced the kind of never-never land in which the sacredness of the Scriptures sometimes tended to immure the figure of Jesus. This represents a great gain.

But is the result pure gain? It would be difficult to say it is. The effect is certainly to restore to Christians the historical Jesus, the Jesus who 'wept'—but what of the Jesus who forgives sins? We have been given a fresh apprehension of the Jesus born in the stable at Bethlehem—but what of the Jesus risen and appearing through the closed doors of the upper room in Jerusalem? Theology has in a sense moved more slowly than art in this matter: the Jesus ethereal, remote and more than a little frigid that appears in the Byzantine tradition of Daphni or the catacomb of Domitilla, in Andrew Rublev or even in Fra Angelico and Fra Lippo Lippi, was replaced as long ago as the Renaissance by Titian's representations of the dimpled smiling infant in the arms of a buxom country wench. The emergence of the historical Jesus raises for theology the question which of these portraits more closely represents the figure of the Gospels and the New Testament generally. Must we not at least say that in the New Testament there are elements that justify both portraits, that criticism has encouraged a too easy acceptance of the second portrait as complete, and that the mysterious Christ has been largely replaced by a merely human Jesus? Treatment of the Bible 'like any other book', then, has led to treatment of Jesus 'like any other man'. But if biblical criticism also sanctioned or even required that the Bible be read in portions, this fragmentation of the record took away the one possible corrective influence. One could not be obliged to take the record as a whole, because it did not in fact constitute a whole. Faith was too easily satisfied with such a discretionary selection from all the material offered by the Gospels as would supply an answer to the inquiry which biblical criticism raises.

2. Form criticism and the person of Jesus

There is almost dramatic excitement as the story of critical biblical study moves into its second phase. A 'startling emphasis on our Lord's humanity' was taken for granted, and more seriously

[1] During the Second World War, an officer censoring British soldiers' letters in Palestine read the following statement: 'When I discovered that I could go by bus to Bethlehem, my faith was shattered.'

than ever before. 'No more Docetism, no more Monophysite explaining away of the human character of the life that Jesus lived, but a full and unreserved recognition of his human nature as "homoousios" with our own, which means "essentially the same as ours": that lesson of the [Jesus of history] movement has been well learnt on all hands, and it is common background today.'[1] 'But,' the same writer goes on, 'at the same time, and even in the same circles, there has emerged another tendency which may seem to point us in an opposite direction, and which certainly carries us far away from what [is] called the "Jesus of history" movement: the tendency to lose interest in the reconstruction of the historical human figure of Jesus.' It would certainly be wrong to interpret what is happening here as simply the swing of the pendulum and the restoration, more or less, of the *status quo ante*. For one thing, this further development is the result of a definable new method of approaching the New Testament and especially the Gospels; and besides, so far from being the consequence of revoking the critical methods already employed in the study of the Bible, the change is due to the extension of these same critical methods, and is only intelligible on the basis of an already accomplished analysis of the records into distinguishable strands and the consequent fragmentation of their unity.

Here too the changed understanding of the Bible brought about a changed representation of the figure of Jesus. The form critics detected in the *Sitz-im-Leben* of the writers of the New Testament records an influence determinative and formative of the documents we now possess. When the canons for careful investigation of the records along these lines are worked out and used,[2] the results are radical. 'We can know almost nothing concerning the life and personality of Jesus,' says Bultmann,[3] 'since the Christian sources show no interest in either, are moreover fragmentary and often legendary; and other sources about Jesus do not exist.' As for the sayings, only a few survive as authentically our Lord's own words. The rest have been so distorted by the influences by means of which they have reached written form that they can no longer be regarded as *ipsissima verba*.

It is fairly easy to see what is happening. Hands went out through the discouraging mists of spiritual exaltation that surrounded the

---

[1] D. M. Baillie, *God was in Christ*, 10.
[2] For an early and one of the clearest statements of the canons used, see R. Bultmann, *Jesus and the Word*, 13.　　　　　　　　　　　　　　　　　　　　[3] Op. cit. 8.

Christ and succeeded in grasping the human Jesus, the Jesus of history. But the impulse got out of control: these same questing hands went further. They attempted to go behind the (when all is said) rather naïve Jesus of history, and groped further—only to find that after all there was nothing tangible on which to lay hold—something hypothetical, perhaps, but certainly almost nothing verifiable. The figure of Jesus had abruptly come to the front of the stage, manifesting full human characteristics—only after a very short time, and at the dictation of those same promoters who had first set him there, to recede again. The methods of form criticism lead to the conclusion that the historical Jesus is beyond recapture. We have Jesus only in record; but the record is so determined and influenced by adventitious factors that much of it cannot be regarded as bearing accurate witness to the main theme of the New Testament at all, and the figure of Jesus withdraws again into obscurity. Thus Bultmann can say:[1] 'Whoever prefers to put the name of "Jesus" always in quotation marks and let it stand as an abbreviation for the historical phenomenon with which we are concerned, is free to do so.' Jesus has retreated to become no more than a mere X, a tenuous and unreal figure, without now even the excuse of sanctity to proffer for his remoteness.

The purpose here does not require us to stop to make a critical assessment of what *Formgeschichte* has done. No doubt the right and most generally accepted course is to say that the critical method it advocates can be employed to yield valuable results, but that restrictions must be imposed upon its use, above all the simple recognition of the fact that the principle of form from which it derives its name is only one among several factors determinative of the composition of the New Testament records. There is, however, an important christological lesson to be learned—one to which attention will have to be more particularly drawn later. Form criticism demonstrates the instability of the concept of the Jesus of history; for when grasped, it seems to crumble away in the hand. This in turn implies that the question which the critical study of the Bible first learnt to put to the records, however valuable the results to which it gave rise, was not calculated to elicit in its completeness the representation of Jesus which these records contain. A specialized treatment had already disturbed the balance of the records, and its preoccupation with what it quite rightly divined to be a real

[1] Op. cit. 14.

interest in the Gospels, their concern with the historicity of the man Jesus, precluded the Gospels from making audible the fuller witness they had to bear to this Jesus.

3. Demythologizing and the person of Jesus

In turning to the debate concerning demythologizing, we have again to disclaim any intention either of presenting a fresh statement of Bultmann's position or of adding another critical commentary of it. The present concern is not with the course of his argument, but with one of its end-products: we have to refer to the form in which eventually the figure of Jesus is presented. But it is as well at the outset to note three things which influence this presentation. (*a*) The first is that Bultmann's aim is genuinely evangelical. He is deeply concerned that no unnecessary impediment to acceptance of the Gospel be placed in the way of modern man. The mythological form given to the original record is such an impediment, but fortunately one that is removable without impairing the essence of the Gospel. Its removal therefore, Bultmann declares, must be effected. (*b*) This does not imply an attempt to render the Gospel palatable to modern man. The Gospel contains an essential element of offence or scandal which cannot be removed. Bultmann's contention is that we have no right to lay upon ourselves or impose on others a non-essential and artificial element of offence. It is clear that, for instance, the phrases in the Creed concerning a descent into hell and an ascent into heaven 'were not a stumbling-block to anyone in the first century', and this 'shows that they are no part of that original *skandalon* which must be retained today'.[1] (*c*) Like the liberals, Bultmann is making use of critical methods. But he breaks decisively with them at two points: first, in desiring not to eliminate elements that do not seem to fit into the portrait of the historical Jesus, but rather to appreciate their essential meaning and to interpret them; and secondly, in the clear affirmation that the essence of Christianity lies not in a teaching but in an event—that in which God decisively does something for us in history in and through Jesus Christ. 'This living Word of God is not invented by

---

[1] See I. Henderson, *Myth in the New Testament*, London 1952, 13 n. 1. Bultmann himself (*Jesus Christ and Mythology*, London 1960, 36) combines these two points when he declares that the aim is to 'eliminate a false stumbling-block and bring into sharp focus the real stumbling-block, the word of the cross.'

the human spirit and by human sagacity; it rises up in history. Its origin is a historical event. . . . This event is Jesus Christ.'[1]

We approach the character of the figure of Jesus which emerges from Bultmann's view by asking about the nature and purpose of the mythological element. Bultmann holds that it is present in the Gospels not in its own right, but for a certain purpose. Mythology, though it takes the form of a certain view of the world, is not really cosmological in origin or intention at all. Though it appears to describe the world, it is in fact really describing man's own existence, and is therefore not so much cosmological as anthropological. 'Myths express the knowledge that man is not master of the world and of his life, that the world within which he lives is full of riddles and mysteries and that human life also is full of riddles and mysteries.'[2] For example, the belief in demons 'is not so much primitive physics or medicine, as man's realisation that his life is limited and conditioned by factors which are beyond his control and which often frustrate his purposes and are essentially indifferent to him.'[3] Hence the expression of the Gospel in mythological terms is simply a device by which it is made to appear relevant to men.

Bultmann illustrates his argument by comparing the case of the man outside with that of the man inside the Christian faith. 'The life of the man without Christ is the life of care and anxiety (*Sorge, Angst*) from which St Paul wished his Corinthian converts to be delivered. When he lives such a life, man is at the mercy of forces indifferent and sometimes hostile to him. . . . He therefore tries to find security in the visible and tangible things of this world. He has, in the words of St Paul, "confidence in the flesh".'[4] But, as in the case of the rich fool in the parable, this security is purely illusory. If he put his trust there, he will be carried away with the world which itself passes away. From this addiction to the things of this world arises also the competition between man and man which leads to hatred, strife, envy and all uncharitableness. Compare with this now the case of the man of faith. He is the man who finds his security in the invisible and not in the visible world. He trusts not in the flesh or any of the furniture of the material world, but in the grace of God which has met him in Jesus Christ. In Bultmann's own words:[5] 'such a life becomes a possession for man through

---

[1] *Jesus Christ and Mythology*, 79.
[2] Ibid. 19.
[3] *Myth in the New Testament*, 14.
[4] Ibid. 15 f.
[5] *Kerygma und Mythos* I, Hamburg 1948, 29, Eng. trs., London 1953, 19 (altered).

faith in God's grace, i.e. through the confidence that the invisible,
the unknown, that which is not at our disposal has met him as love
and opened up a future for him which signifies not death but life.'
This life has the quality of forgiveness, in that he is freed from his
past and from his past addiction to the things of this world; and
also of obedience, for he is thus freed for life with God and for
service of him. 'He has power over the things of the world, but they
no longer have power over him.'[1] This is the essence of the Gospel,
and clearly it applies to all men at all times whether they believe in
actual demons or not.

The figure of Jesus then appears as follows. Jesus is indeed the
carpenter of Nazareth as represented in the Gospel stories. But
interwoven with the presentation of this figure are elements incongruous with a mere Nazareth carpenter. He works miracles, he is
credited with pre-existence, and so on. These are mythical elements
inserted not for their own sake, but to bring out the fact that this
historical figure is not merely a historical figure, but is the way
whereby God has enabled us to make the transition from our fallen
or unauthentic existence. 'The motive of the mythological treatment
of Christ was [Bultmann considers] to draw attention to, and to
attempt to make credible, the fact that this particular historical event
of the life and death of Jesus is eschatological,'[2] that is, really calls
men into the new life by placing before them an inescapable
decision.

The Heideggerian philosophy in terms of which this view of
Jesus Christ is worked out deals in greater detail and in philosophical terms with the human predicament and with the remedy
Christianity proposes. With this we are not essentially concerned
here. It is enough to say that the event of Jesus in his life and death
is the presentation to man of a genuinely alternative understanding
of his being. In him, a man sees what authentic being is, and this
alternative is presented to him as a live option. It becomes a live
option because Christ's life and death is to be regarded not as
merely occurring in history some 1900 years ago, but also as relevant
and all-important for the lives of men today. It is, as Bultmann
says, *eschatologisch*, not merely *historisch* but *geschichtlich*. As he
says:[3] 'The cross and passion are therefore present realities. How
little they are to be confined to the events of the first Good Friday

---

[1] *Myth in the New Testament*, 16.   [2] Ibid. 48.
[3] *Kerygma und Mythos*, 43, Eng. trs. 37 (altered).

is apparent from the words which a disciple of St Paul represents
him as using: "who now rejoice in my sufferings for you, and fill
up that which is behind of the afflictions of Christ in my flesh for
his body's sake, which is the church" (Col. 1.24).'

Of the part which man is called upon to play if this live option
is to be effective, we shall have to speak at a later point in the
argument. We ask here concerning the character with which the
figure of Jesus Christ is represented. Bultmann's contention is[1] that
'unless the Child had been born, I should not have come to this new
and true understanding of myself'. The real difficulty here is that
what saves is this true knowledge of myself. Certainly, since this
knowledge involves decision, knowledge of our being is an integral
part of our being, and a change there is really a change here, a new
understanding is a new me. But it also remains true that this
knowledge, one must think, was in some sense mine all the time.
Not, as Thielicke points out,[2] that it is mine in an autogenetical
(*autogenetisch*) or Socratic way. 'It needs an event to bring it to
birth'; or again, it is there waiting to be deistically 'cranked up'
(*angekurbelt*) by God working in history in Jesus. Jesus is then no
more than the imparter of this knowledge or the occasion on which
this knowledge comes to be apprehended. Then his place is neither
permanent nor indispensable; it is only (as is that of any teacher)
introductory to that which is the real agent of salvation. So Thielicke
fears a 'palace revolution' in which those who have been made
beneficiaries of this knowledge will shake themselves loose from
him who let them into its secret. Certainly Jesus is not locked away
in the past, but comes to challenge each individual. But this is in
the last resort to make of him nothing more than a 'permanent
possibility' of salvation.

An intention good in itself has thus reached a conclusion which
is meagre. That an event of the utmost importance occurred in the
appearance of Jesus Christ is established. But the exigencies of
demythologizing preclude us from saying very much about the
content of this event, and from saying almost anything about him
who came. The simplest and most memorable example of the
mythology that has to be discarded is the famous 'three-decker
universe' in terms of which the Gospel story is told. Has Bultmann
rightly assessed the difficulty which this presents to the ordinary

[1] *Myth in the New Testament*, 39 f.
[2] *Kerygma und Mythos*, 167, Eng. trs. 148.

man of today? Is it not an exaggeration to make out that this is really an insuperable obstacle to his acceptance of the Gospel? May we not say that he is in fact able and indeed willing to see *through* it? Corroboration that this is so may be found in the following consideration. By a certain natural necessity, we think of God as being above us, and feel it inappropriate to conceive him as below us.[1] This is practically exemplified in the naturalness with which we kneel down before God in prayer (Ps. 95.6), or stand with the head bowed (Luke 18.13). This seems to imply that religion is necessarily mythological in character, and that religious language is ineradicably mythopoeic. At the cost of emphasizing in an exaggerated way an element that must be taken into account in any Christology, biblical criticism reminds us that Jesus Christ is at least truly human. But if so, he enters into this aspect of the human situation as well as others. The Bible therefore talks of 'humbling himself' (Phil. 2.8) and even more explicitly of 'descending' (Eph. 4.9 f., cf. John 6.41, 50, 58); and on the other hand of his 'ascending' (Eph. 4.9 f., cf. Luke 24.51; Acts 1.9) to exaltation. It is the measure of the full condescension to a human condition that comes to expression here. And, so far from finding insuperable difficulty in the concepts, the ordinary man can and would use no others. If this is a 'category' native to humanity, then it is of the greatest importance that it should not be regarded as imposed upon Christ by subjective interpretation, but that it should really be assumed by him. The attempt to divest the figure of Jesus Christ of such modes of presentation rests upon the assumption that such temporal and spatial modes are an essential handicap. But is this not exactly parallel to saying that Jesus' body was a handicap, and does not this in turn imperil the reality of the incarnation?

If this is so, what Bultmann has done in portraying the figure of Jesus is not to admire the mystery of the incarnation with awe, but to shy away from it as an offence. Jesus is no more than he was presented by Bultmann in the earlier form-critical stage of his development—an X; and the only difference is that this X is now

---

[1] A loose parallel may be suggested. We speak of high and low notes in music, of a singer who 'reaches up' to achieve a top note, and so on; and we do this fully aware that physical height and depth are not categories that accurately apply. An even more light-hearted parallel is suggested by a consideration made by E. H. Gombrich, *Art and Illusion*, New York 1960). If 'ping' and 'pong' were the only words we had, and we had to name an elephant and a cat, which would be ping and which pong? Everyone answers this question in the same way. When, he adds, we know why 'o' sounds 'heavier' than 'i', a good many mysteries will be resolved.

represented in such a way as to offer men, on condition of their right decision, an entry into the authentic being which is identical with salvation.

4. The person of Jesus in criticism and the 'in Christ'

From Glover's *Jesus of History*[1] to Bultmann's 'Jesus the un-known X'—it is indeed a long road that has been travelled between these two points; and that the same road should have led to such unexpected conclusions adds to its interest. The conclusions themselves have aroused widespread controversy, into which we do not need to enter here. But it is worth while asking whether literary criticism, form criticism and demythologizing, if they signify three stages on the same road, and if they together lead to an erroneous conclusion, have some error in common which has lain undetected.

There can be no doubt about the sincerity and good intentions of those who travelled this way. The venture was fundamentally an honest attempt to apply to the basis of the Christian faith principles which had been used elsewhere with outstanding success. It is quite true that in the first stage of the process some of the results of criticism were accepted with delight by the opponents of Christianity; and it is also true that what was going on in the name of criticism left a deposit of doubt in the minds of ordinary Christians. But the attempt made by some Roman Catholic writers to represent the movement as a gigantic anti-Christian conspiracy was neither convincing nor successful; and the attitude of detachment and opposition shown by the Roman Church to the study being conducted within what it called 'modernism' was unfortunate.[2] In any case, by the time the second stage is reached, it is clearly not the unbelieving critic that is forcing the pace, but thinkers who stand within the membership of the Christian Church. What confronts us here therefore may or may not be heresy; but at least it is not an intentional denial of the foundations of the Christian faith.

One thing at least is clear: Jesus Christ as represented at each of the three stages is unable to support the function allotted to him

[1] The famous book first published in London in 1917; ten years later it was in its nineteenth impression.

[2] C. J. Cadoux, *Catholicism and Christianity*, London 1928, and A. R. Vidler, *The Modernist Movement in the Roman Church*, Cambridge 1934, give Protestant versions of the story; the Roman version, as given e.g. in *Divino Afflante Spiritu* §45, is naturally rather different.

E

if we are to use the phrase 'in Christ' at all. The Christ left in our hands when the literary critics have done their work is certainly credited with a human nature and all the characteristics of humanity can properly be attributed to it. Either this representation is regarded as exhaustively expressing what the Gospels themselves have to say; or it is regarded as the residuary essential core when the Gospel account has been stripped of subsequent theological and dogmatic accretions. On the first view, there can be no ground for speaking of 'in Christ' that is stronger and more compelling than in the case of anyone else. Adventitious reasons may make it desirable to have such contact with him rather than with any other; but nothing said about his nature supplies a reason why the same relation as that designated by 'in Christ' should not be asserted of other human beings. On the other view, it is admitted that the Christ of the Gospels does appear to be credited with a more than human nature. Of this evidence no use is made—and for an assignable reason. The reason is that the evidence is attributable to later reflection on and development of the simple portrait at the heart of the authentic Gospel, an influence most clearly exemplified outside the Gospels in St Paul and the other parts of the New Testament. Hence it is impossible to establish an identity between the true and historical Jesus and the theological Christ of later Christian thought. A fatal gap has opened up between the Christ of the Gospels and the exalted Christ who meets St Paul on the Damascus road and with whom, on the Pauline witness, contact is still made in the 'in Christ'.

Application of the 'in Christ' to the figure represented by form criticism also reveals defect. The Christ who is elicited from the Gospel records has lost his grip upon historical humanity. He is, the conclusion runs, largely the construct of the mind of the primitive Church. It is, however, not denied that the primitive Church was guided by the Holy Spirit in so developing its picture of Christ out of the simpler historical Jesus. We have thus some kind of acknowledgment of the Christ in us, and of his Church being gradually conformed to the mind which was in Christ Jesus. But St Paul speaks not only of Christ being in us, but of us being 'in Christ', and of this essential supplement in the Pauline thought not a trace is left. St Paul thinks not merely of Christ in me eliciting subjective apprehension of the sublimity of his person. He also holds that such transference or change of status has taken place that I may be said to be 'in Christ'. This is only conceivable on the basis of an assured humanity, and of this humanity form criticism has undermined all assurance.

To this may be added the comment applicable to the demythologizing venture. If in the case of the form critics there is retained the Christ in me, though the I 'in Christ' is lost, it would appear that the consequence of demythologizing is the loss of both. Bultmann's representation cannot bridge the discrepancy between the exemplary but unknown X who realizes true human potentiality and so vindicates it as a human possibility, and the state in which men are left if no more than a possibility, however attractive and however encouragingly presented, is offered to them by Christ. Too much is then left for fallen man to do, if Christ does not do more for them than this.

5. *A wrong treatment of the New Testament witness*

The diagnosis that seems best to fit the facts is that the New Testament documents have been approached in the wrong manner, treated in a way which results in the distortion of what they have to say, and asked questions to which answers were extorted rather than found. If the venture has to be regarded as undertaken in good faith, it also has the initial appearance of being laudable and useful. *Post eventum*, however, it is possible to see why the prosecution of this venture in and by itself alone was no more than dubiously valid. The attempt rests on the assumption that the New Testament record is constituted by two elements which are not only separable but really separate. There is the primary datum which is the Jesus of history, and beyond this there is the element of interpretation imposed on this datum. This second element when separated off from the historical datum must find its ground elsewhere, and this elsewhere can only be in the mind and spiritual reflection of the early witnesses. This works itself out in exactly these terms in the sequel: the primary datum was in fact found to have a good deal of matter embedded in it that was contributed from other sources, and when this had been discarded little enough remained of the Jesus of history. Finally, even this little was diminished still further when it was suggested not only that this saying or that recorded deed were suspect, but that the whole intellectual framework of the day infected all that could be said and recorded with such

temporality and transience as to render all but a very small essential
kernel invalid for a later age. For the venture of demythologizing,
'the event,' says Thielicke, 'is not the Jesus of history, but Jesus
valued as the Christ.'[1] The initial assumption thus contrived a
devastating revenge. The primary historical datum when split off
from the New Testament records is unable to support itself, and
suffers progressive diminution until virtually vanishing point is
reached.

'The Bible must be studied "like any other book" '—but must it,
and can it? If it cannot be so studied, is there an alternative method
of study which is proper to it? 'These are written,' says the writer
of the Fourth Gospel about what he has deliberately chosen to set
down (John 20.31), 'that ye may believe.' This represents a starting-
point different from that just considered and quite incongruous with
it. It is true that this simple statement is itself capable of varying
interpretations. It can be understood to mean that such things have
been set down, either such remembered facts or such factitious
reflections or perhaps both, as would induce the state of belief. But,
it is to be noted, this understanding already reads into the writer's
mind that dislocation of fact from interpretation which was the
presupposition of the recovery and then in turn of the loss of the
historical Jesus. There is a simpler possible explanation of what
the writer here says. It is that what he records is an order of things in
which fact and interpretation are interlocked and both equally and
inseparably belong to the datum; this is what constitutes the Gospel,
and it is this that he will set down and transmit. From this point of
view, the procedure adopted by those interested in the Jesus of
history must lead to a different result from that contemplated by the
writer of the Gospel, and this is only another way of saying that it
leads to error. For what is undertaken by them is a disintegration
of the primary witness and a consequent dismantling into discrete
elements of what primitively was held together. The responsibility
of justifying this dismemberment is to be laid on the shoulders of
those who practise it, as does also the duty of defining and of
observing the limits within which it may properly be done. We may
put the matter in other terms. Granted that the New Testament
witness is a compound of elements; how is it to be understood?
Either the unity or the diversity is primary. If the diversity, it looks
as if the conclusions reached in the course of criticism will be

[1] *Kerygma und Mythos*, 166 n. 1, Eng. trs. 147 n. 1.

irresistible. If on the other hand it is the unity that is prior, the attempt made to establish an independent Jesus of history represents a subtraction from the New Testament Jesus Christ, and it does not appear that this subtraction can at a later stage be made good. Only if it be remembered that it is an abstraction can the work of criticism be prevented from leading to conclusions which are not merely arid, and not merely unorthodox, but which make it impossible to see how it comes about that there is a Gospel to preach at all.

6. *Unity of fact and interpretation*

Attention has been recently drawn to what has here been called the unity of fact and interpretation contained in the primitive record of the Gospel. Hoskyns[1] twenty years ago said that the 'historical Jesus is the place in history where it is demanded that men should believe—and where they can so easily disbelieve, but where, if they disbelieve, the concrete history is found to be altogether meaningless, and where, if they believe, the fragmentary story of his life is woven into one whole, manifesting the glory of God and the glory of men who have been created by him.' At this point, fact and interpretation, history and faith, stand together. Brunner[2] draws the distinction between the Christ 'in the flesh' and the Christ 'after the flesh', and thinks that the failure to do so is paralleled by a 'perversion of faith in the supposed interests of historicity. Faith,' he goes on to say, 'never arises out of the observation of facts, but out of the Word of God. This Word of God, however, has certainly come "into the flesh", and is thus connected with observation.' And again: 'The forgiving love of God cannot become real to us without the picture of this event, nor can the story of this event convey to us the forgiveness of God apart from this Word. The doctrine is the story and the story is the doctrine. Hence it is esoteric history, which will not disclose its meaning to any mere historian, and esoteric doctrine which no philosopher can understand.'[3] So too Karl Barth[4] in 1957 is found saying: 'In the first

[1] E. C. Hoskyns, *The Fourth Gospel*, London 1940, Introduction §IV, 'The Historical Tension of the Fourth Gospel', 91, quoted by D. M. MacKinnon, 'Philosophy and Christology', in *Essays in Christology for Karl Barth*, ed. T. H. L. Parker, London 1956, 293.
[2] E. Brunner, *The Mediator*, Eng. trs., London 1934, 160.
[3] Ibid. 521.
[4] *Evangelische Theologie im 19. Jahrhundert* (Theologische Studien, Heft 49. Zollikon-Zürich 1957), 21, Eng. trs., *God, Grace and Gospel* (*Scottish Journal of Theology*, Occasional Papers no. 8), Edinburgh 1959, 71 f. Barth in fact extends this idea to all history:

New Testament attestations to this faith and also in the later attestations by the Church, with all their diversity and temporal conditioning, was he to be conceived otherwise than as its ground, object and content? Was therefore his historical existence one that was generally accessible to a research which went behind the texts of the New Testament? Did these texts not possess a structure which made them useless as a "source" which could be employed by neutral historical science?' H. Diem[1] points out that there is 'an interweaving of "historical" and "unhistorical" elements, i.e. of the history that can be established as true by the ordinary methods of historical inquiry, and of such as cannot be so established.' But an even greater witness can be cited: the connection between faith and understanding is expressed by our Lord himself when (John 8.43) he distinguishes between *logos* and *lalia*: 'Why do ye not understand my speech? even because ye cannot hear my word!'[2] So closely are the two elements to be held together that only the word can give meaning to the speech. This means that the overt and sensible, the apparent and historical, cannot even be said to make up an intelligible story by themselves alone. Only when illuminated by the *logos* does it acquire meaning.

7. 'In Christ' implies Christ's real humanity, past and present

At an earlier point in this chapter, the formula 'in Christ' was applied in a summary fashion to the three stages of the theological development which has been under examination. The application revealed at least some of the defects of the view of Christ which is represented at each of the stages mentioned. The formula must now

'History as a whole is always partly unhistorical, history as a whole can only be described as unhistorical, inasmuch as God's creative action is always at work in the whole process of history, and history as a whole, in all its movements, relations and forms, always has an aspect by which it is immediately related to God and is of immediate divine ordinance. And how can we overlook the fact that in the last resort all history is truly important and significant only in so far as it has this element, in so far as it is not merely historical but also unhistorical? How could we forget that all historical writing must be unreasonable and profitless to the extent that it proposes to speak only in historical terms and not also unhistorically?' One could think that rather more thought has to be given to this obliteration of the distinction between 'sacred' and other history; for, if the distinction is real and yet is not preserved in this way, some other terms will have to be found in which it may be expressed. Cf. the modern discussion of the validity of the idea of *Heilsgeschichte*.

[1] H. Diem, *Dogmatics*, Eng. trs., Edinburgh 1959, 95; cf. *Theologie als kirchliche Wissenschaft* Band I, Exegese und Historie, Munich 1952, 107 ff.

[2] See T. F. Torrance, 'The Place of Christology', in *Essays in Christology for Karl Barth*, 28.

be applied with greater rigour to the question of the person of Christ, with the intention of eliciting some of the features that any valid representation of Christ must properly manifest.

It may be well to draw attention to a distinction between two closely similar phrases: the Jesus of history and the historical Jesus. For much of this chapter we have been looking at the view represented by the first of these phrases, and observing the momentous consequences that flow from it. The conception of the Jesus of history comes under a cloud of suspicion. But this must by no means be understood to imply either that Christianity can dispense with, or that the point of view represented here is indifferent to, the historical ties which at the incarnation were assumed. Christianity has a deep and inalienable interest in a historical Jesus. This conception, in contrast to that of the Jesus of history, does justice to the orthodox view that, while Jesus was in history, he was not embedded or submerged in history. He indeed is historical, but he is not only or even primarily historical. Failure to reckon with this distinction accounts, one must suppose, for the reiterated attribution to Karl Barth of a lack of interest in the humanity of Jesus.

We have now to ask the question whether the 'in Christ' throws any light upon the nature of this historical Jesus. If we may be said to be in Christ, what are we thereby required to think concerning his nature? If the 'in Christ' is to mean anything, we must be talking about a Christ with an incontestable humanity—a historical Christ, though not a Jesus of history. If this were not so, then one of two consequences would seem to follow. On the one hand, in order to be in him, we should have to be translated into another and non-human mode of being, quite different from that which as men we possess. This would be pressing the view that salvation means rescue out of the world to lengths at which it becomes plainly untenable. It is quite true that we are men properly speaking only as we are in him. But then there is an improper way of being man which is none the less quite real. It will not therefore do to construe the nature of Christ in such a way that in order to be in him we have simply to forsake our humanity. And if this is so, then we must hold two things. We must hold that the Christ in whom we are said to be not only now has a humanity in which we may participate; we must also hold that this humanity is that which as incarnate he displayed in the days of his flesh. On the other hand, unless it is real humanity that Christ had and has, the alternative

consequence to which we should be led is that in being in Christ
we are given another nature alongside our humanity. But this would
clearly not save us as men, since the humanity we still possess would
remain untouched; and being thus untouched, according to the
rubric of Gregory of Nazianzus, τὸ ἀπρόσληπτον ἀθεράπευτον, it would
be unsaved.

Mention has already been made that this is the erroneous consequence that follows from the tendency apparent in both Deissmann
and Weiss to spiritualize the Christ in whom we are said to be. To
speak at this point of atmosphere and of the air we breathe to help
out our understanding of what happens when a man is in Christ is
all very well, provided that it is clearly understood that we are
speaking in figurative and metaphorical terms. But to construe the
Christ with whom salvific contact is made in these terms is really
to give us a Christ who is disabled from helping us wholly as we
now are.

Can we say anything further about this requirement which the
'in Christ' demands? There is, we may say, a static and an active
aspect to be taken into account. 'When the fulness of time was
come, God sent forth his Son, made of a woman' (Gal. 4.4). These
words are determinative of the humanity which our Lord assumed
for us men and for our salvation. It is our humanity that he wears.
Here we must reflect on what was said in an earlier chapter. The
humanity we have is ambiguous: it is possible for us either to be or
not to be a man. It is this in all its ambiguity that our Lord takes on
himself in the birth at Bethlehem. Otherwise we should have no
part in him. But to this must be added at once the active aspect. Just
as it is characteristic of us that by ourselves we incline not to be man
and so forfeit the estate for which we have been made and to which
we are called, so it is characteristic of Christ that he successfully
preserves his human nature in that relationship to God in which
alone it attains and retains the true being of humanity. In his active
obedience displayed throughout his earthly life, he perfectly con-
serves the true filial relationship to the Father, and against all
temptation could at the last offer the perfect sacrifice of an obedient
life. As St Bernard says: *non mors sed oboedentia morientis Deo
placuit.*

In a passage of special interest, T. F. Torrance has recently made
this point with great force:[1] 'It was in his flesh (our humanity which

[1] T. F. Torrance, *The School of Faith*, London 1959, lxxxi ff.

he assumed) that he was anointed, and in his flesh that he has accomplished all the parts of our salvation. Thus in virtue of his incarnation and his saving work, Christ has eternal life and salvation residing in himself, that is, even in his human nature. . . . By his human nature Christ exerts saving influence upon us.' As Torrance goes on to say, this is quite unintelligible for the liberal theology that talked so much, but without sufficient profundity, of the historical life of Jesus.

Unless this humanity is carried by him into his exalted life, there can be no 'in Christ' available for us. But here we are being carried forward to consideration of the work of Christ, which is the subject to be next considered.

The present chapter may close with a reference to a recent little book by Werner Pelz.[1] 'Biologically speaking, I am not made out of nothing. But the "I" that can say "I", the "I" burdened and warped by ages of unbelief, the "I" called into freedom, that "I" comes out of nothing.' One cannot feel entirely happy about this way of putting the matter. If 'the "I" that says "I" ' simply 'comes out of nothing', how does it come about that unfailingly this 'I' is still subject to sin and the agent of sinful acts? Nevertheless, the sentiment may stand as a statement of the essential dependence and independence which characterize the individual in responsible conduct. But it may also be applied to the nature of Christ. Christ too has causal physical antecedents—'born of the Virgin Mary'; and in his case, the 'I' that says 'I' does not come out of nothing: 'I proceeded forth and came from God' (John 8.42). Of the Christ who was before the incarnation takes place, it cannot be said that we are in him;[2] of the Christ who after the incarnation returns to the Father (John 14.12; 16.10), it cannot but be said.

---

[1] Werner Pelz, *Irreligious Reflections on the Christian Church*, London 1959, 91.

[2] At least in no ordinary sense. Some theologians have ventured to attribute to Christ the possession of a pre-incarnate humanity, for example the Quaker writers Isaac Penington and George Keith. The latter speaks of a 'pre-existent heavenly humanity of Christ' and bases the idea especially on John 6.31 and I Cor. 10.3 f. (*The Way Cast Up*, London 1677); while the former talks of a 'prepared body' or, as he says, 'veil', for which he cites Heb. 10.5 ('A Question to the Professors of Christianity', *Works*, vol. II, London 1681, 14 *et al.*), itself based upon the misleading LXX of Ps. 40.6. This is not an easy conception, and it is difficult to reconcile with the genuine novelty which occurs in the nativity of our Lord. On the other hand, it cannot be supposed that the assumption of humanity at the incarnation was such a novelty for the pre-existent Christ as (if we may put it so) to catch him by surprise.

4

The Impartation of the Life

1. *God's part and man's*

IF the 'in Christ' throws light on the christological problem of the nature of Jesus Christ, it may be expected to do no less in respect of the soteriological problem of the work of Jesus Christ. For a first statement of the problem to be considered here, a quotation may be cited. 'The Christian believes that God has shown himself to human beings who could never have discovered him for themselves; that he has forgiven them before they asked forgiveness; that he has removed the barriers from his side, so that they need only to accept what has already been made available for them—reconciliation with himself. Yet there is much concealed in the phrase "need only to accept", for it is precisely this which all men find impossible. The Christian also believes that God himself makes this acceptance possible.'[1] The question posed here is one that is familiar, recurrent and profound. It concerns the relations of God and man, and in particular the parts played by God and man in what is done if men are to be saved.

The issue is a contemporary one. For the question of the meaning of faith has recently moved into the forefront of discussion. Theologians have been talking about the statements of faith with the philosophers,[2] and also about the nature and source of religious and

---

[1] 'What do Christians mean by Salvation?' by Principal Frederic Greeves, in *The Student Movement*, Christmas 1959, 8.

[2] The reference is of course to the dialogue between the philosophy of linguistic analysis and theology, represented for example in such books as *Metaphysical Beliefs* by S. E. Toulmin, R. W. Hepburn and A. MacIntyre (London 1957) and *Faith and Logic*, edited by Basil Mitchell (London 1957), and also more recently W. F. Zuurdeeg, *An Analytical Philosophy of Religion* (London 1959). It may be that the discussion has made its contribution and has not much longer to run. Professor A. J. Ayer in a review of Ernest Gellner's *Words and Things* (London 1959) in an issue of the *Spectator* (December 1959) wrote: 'The fact is that linguistic philosophy was taken up in England just because it was not thought to be useless. Its attraction lay in its appearing to be an avenue of philosophic progress. This may have become a blind alley; I am inclined to think that it has. But this is not an excuse for imputing frivolity to those who pursue it.'

especially Christian faith among themselves. Those who contribute to the latter conversation have much in common. It is agreed that faith is a human activity of some kind—men do, or of course do not, manifest or have faith. Most people further would hold that faith has the character of response. But response is a relative term, demanding a correlate, and this by general agreement also is found in God, faith being in some sense God-given. At this point arises the issue which thrusts theologians apart and forces them to take sides. How does a man have faith as his own response, while at the same time it is given to him by God? In what relation do men and God stand in the matter of faith? Evidently sides may here be taken: there are those who lay emphasis on faith being really a man's own —his own contribution, as it may be put, to religion; others require the thing to be differently stated and insist upon the divine givenness of faith. These two attitudes may now be illustrated.

2. *An existentialist answer : Bultmann*

Adopting the first attitude are those who have been more or less influenced by existentialism. In existentialism, it is felt, there is emphasized an element essential to the Christian faith which in the theological account of Christianity is all too easily obscured or even obliterated. Christianity is not merely a matter of subscribing, or giving *assensus*, to *the faith*. No doubt this element has its precedent in the New Testament, and for James 'faith means mere intellectual assent to a proposition, such as that God is one' (James 2.19).[1] But this has to be supplemented by, and understood in the light of, the Pauline witness. In I Cor. 1.21–29, St Paul requires Jews and Greeks to choose between the wisdom and strength that are divine in origin and those which have a human basis. In saying this, St Paul is flanked both earlier and later by indubitable evidence that intellectual assent to a *depositum fidei* is not all that faith involves. There is a repeated dominical emphasis on the need for choice. Men have to make their choice between God and mammon (Matt. 6.24); their house must be built either on the rock or on the sand (Matt. 7.24–27); they are either to lose their life by saving it or to save it by losing it (Mark. 8.35). The *hic et nunc* character of the demand comes to powerful expression in the case of the rich young ruler, willing enough to obey the decalogue, but declining to commit himself to

[1] See *The Teacher's Commentary*, London 1955, 505.

the particular action demanded (Matt. 19.16–22). And the practical repercussions of the greatest question of all, 'Whom do ye say that I am?' (Matt. 16.15), are plain for all to see. Nor does this note die away in the post-Pauline period: a strict reprimand is administered to the Church of Laodicea (Rev. 2.14–18) for its relapse into what Bultmann would call 'unauthentic being',[1] and an uncompromising choice is put before it. The statement of this element in the Christian faith by means of the terminology of existentialism amounts to a rediscovery and is a notable feature of modern theological thought. 'Existentialism has performed a valuable service in recalling Christians to an awareness of this truth, for it is a truth that they can easily forget.'[2]

The form in which the existentialist emphasis is most formidably expressed is that recently given to it by Rudolf Bultmann. For Bultmann, 'the act of faith is an act of choice and a *concrete* act of choice'; and in this, says a recent commentator,[3] 'Bultmann will win widespread agreement'. This may be so, but those from whom the agreement is won should be aware of the hazardous implications that are thereby incurred. In Bultmann's case, at any rate, these implications become plain. What is offered to man by Christ is the 'possibility of a new life which has to be appropriated by deliberate resolve'.[4] Again, commenting on Gal. 5.16, he says that the life of the believer consists in 'the constant appropriation of grace by faith, which also means, in the concrete "obedience" which is henceforth possible in his walking'.[5] Thus 'the indicative "You are in the Spirit" becomes "God forgives sins through Christ", and the imperative "Walk according to the Spirit" becomes "Appropriate God's forgiveness through deliberate resolve".'[6] It appears therefore that the whole matter turns upon man's appropriation, whether it be stated in scriptural terms as the appropriation of the forgiveness made available for us in Christ, or in existentialist terms as the choice of that possibility of authentic being of which Christ is the egregious example.[7]

The proximate cause of Bultmann's restatement of the Christian faith in these terms is certainly his expressed affirmation that the

---

[1] See H. P. Owen, *Revelation and Existence*, Cardiff 1957, 74 n. 3.
[2] Ibid. 74.   [3] Ibid. 75.   [4] *Kerygma and Myth*, 121.
[5] *Theology of the New Testament* I, Eng. trs. by K. Grobel, London 1952, 274-9.
[6] *Revelation and Existence*, 76.
[7] Christ, to use the words of Romain Gary in his novel *The Roots of Heaven* (London 1958), may be said to 'have proved that to be a man was after all a possible endeavour'; but it is still up to us to realize this possibility.

concept of Spirit has to be demythologized. When this is done, there remains no indwelling power which can be adduced as the guarantee (see II Cor. 1.22, 5.5, where St Paul calls the Spirit ἀρραβών) of salvation. As Paul Althaus says,[1] according to Bultmann, 'I am confronted with a decision, I am questioned, I must answer; but of the power that can compel me to believe, there is not a word.' All therefore hangs upon the ability of men to lay hold on what is offered. They must bring to the matter a deliberate choice and, unaided by any other supernatural agency, must appropriate what is held out to them.

In fact, all those who are committed to the existentialist emphasis upon choice, whether they reject the method of demythologizing or not, have their feet upon the same road. It is up to man to take what is offered; and, since on the existentialist view man's essence consists not in a being but in a programme,[2] the deliberate resolve to do so must emanate exclusively from himself; for otherwise man would be other than essentially he is. The existentialist view of man commits him to a kind of choice for which there are no extrinsic aids. If this is true, however salutary the emphasis upon the need for choice in the making of a Christian, the element has become so disproportionately large as to disturb the balance which St Paul carefully maintains. For he even-handedly lays an emphasis also upon the action of God: 'By grace are ye saved through faith; and that not of yourselves: it is the gift of God' (Eph. 2.8). The clear testimony of Scripture is that God operates even at the point where men in faith accept the benefits Christ offers.

3. An existentialist answer: Tillich

From a rather different standpoint, Tillich moves in a direction and to an end fundamentally similar. 'Faith,' he repeats over and over again,[3] 'is the state of being ultimately concerned.' Everyone knows the difficulty of knowing quite what is being said when the terminology used is as individual as that of Tillich. As it stands, the phrase might be quite satisfactory. Undoubtedly it does convey something of both the urgency and the personal character of faith, and thus does duty for what the language of the existentialists so

---

[1] The So-called Kerygma and the Historical Jesus, Eng. trs., Edinburgh 1959, 46.
[2] The phrase is of course Jean-Paul Sartre's.
[3] E.g. in Dynamics of Faith, London 1957, 1, 4, with variations on the phrase passim.

emphatically and up to a point rightly expresses. But it is not clear that he succeeds in avoiding the hazards to which we have seen they are exposed, or even that he is conscious that there are hazards. Doubts begin to gather about this definition of faith as the exposition proceeds. Here four points may be noted. (a) First, the definition is reinforced by, though we may not say based upon, analogy with things other than men. 'Man, like every living thing, is concerned about many things, above all about those which condition his very existence, such as food and shelter.'[1] This similarity is apparently worth mentioning, although there is also a 'contrast' to which attention is drawn. But the same 'concern' is found in both contexts. The implication is that the faith that is here being defined has similarity to, if not its roots in, the concern which every living thing manifests. (b) Secondly, the argument continues,[2] 'man, in contrast to other living beings, has spiritual concerns—cognitive, aesthetic, social, political.' These concerns differ from one another in urgency, and each of them 'can claim ultimacy for a human life or the life of a social group'. If this, then, is the basis of faith, it is to be found apparently exactly where a number of concerns other than it jostle one another with competing claims. Of course this does full justice to what is commonly said, that e.g. nationalism can and often does take the place of religion, thrusting it, along with 'all other concerns, economic well-being, health and life, family, aesthetic and cognitive truth, justice and humanity' on one side by its ruthless exclusiveness. Yet it is one thing to say that religion can be and often is smothered to the point of extinction by a surrogate religion such as nationalism; it is quite another to affirm that the concern which is faith is on a level with this other successful rival concern. (c) That it is the second and not the first of these affirmations that Tillich is making appears from the third point to be noted. Idolatrous faith consists, he declares, in being ultimately concerned about something ultimately unable to sustain it and hence disruptive of personality. It is, that is to say, one manifestation belonging to the same species as religious faith. The question immediately arises whether this is really the case. Would it not be nearer the truth to say that in the Bible idolatrous faith is precisely that which arises from human concern? and must not the God that answers to this concern be the artefact of which St Paul speaks in Rom. 1.23? (d) If there are doubts whether this is what Tillich is

[1] Op. cit. 1.   [2] Loc. cit.

saying, the fourth point seems to clear them up. 'The content [of faith],' he says, 'matters infinitely for the life of the believer, but it does not matter for the formal definition of faith. And this is the first step we have to make in order to understand the dynamics of faith.'[1] The thought then is clear. Concern is a basic characteristic of men along with other living beings, and it is this that gives rise to faith. Into this formal human characteristic various substantive contents can be fitted, while faith remains the same. Different kinds of faith differ only according to the different content which each embraces.

Clearly we are dealing here with an anthropocentric understanding of what faith means. This account with great acuteness and profound insight lays down the conditions existing in man which make the rise of faith possible. But when the work is done, there is little or no room for any extrinsic agent to evoke it. In a manner of speaking, the response is already being made, awaiting something to which it can be given. If this is true, it is more than difficult to find any place or meaning in the frequent references in Scripture to the new thing that is brought into being by the work of Christ.

It is only fair to add that Tillich elsewhere goes some way towards correcting a balance not always preserved in what he says. Dealing with what he calls 'the correlation between existentialist questions and theological answers', he is willing to take revelation with great seriousness. 'God,' he says,[2] 'is manifest only through God.' He goes on: 'The existential question, namely, man himself in the conflicts of his existential situation, is not the source for the revelatory answer formulated by theology. One cannot derive the divine self-manifestation from an analysis of the human predicament'; and he is willing to concede that 'theological supernaturalism, as represented, for example, by contemporary neo-orthodoxy, is right in asserting the inability of man to reach God under his own power.'[3] Yet the anthropological bias in his thought is apparent even here. Man apparently knows God at least under the form of a question; as he says: 'Man as man knows the question of God.' And again: 'Man is the question, not the answer. It is equally wrong to derive the question implied in human existence from the revelatory answer.'[4] But if faith is basically the same and varies only

---

[1] Op. cit. 4. [2] *Systematic Theology* II, Eng. trs., London 1957, 75.
[3] Ibid. 14 f. [4] Ibid. 15.

in the content with which it is filled, how is the question man
knows 'the question of *God*'? how is it a question with any specific
character at all? how is it anything more than a question mark
before which a number of different but equally appropriate terms
can be placed?

4. *The Barthian retort*

A quite different view of faith is offered by those who like Karl
Barth emphasize its divine character. In fact the transition to this
other attitude has already been prepared in what has just been said.
In a long subsection entitled 'The Readiness of Man', contained in
a volume of the *Kirchliche Dogmatik* which cites the name of
Tillich only once and that for a quite subsidiary purpose,[1] Barth
propounds a view which is point for point at variance with what
Tillich says. The contrariety is not without its occasional resemblance. The thesis stated at the head of the section[2] reads: 'The
possibility of the knowledge of God springs from God, in that he is
himself the truth and gives himself to man in his Word by the Holy
Spirit to be known as the truth.' There, however, similarity between
the two views ends; for the statement continues: 'It springs from
man in that, in the Son of God by the Holy Spirit, he becomes an
object of the divine good pleasure and therefore participates in the
truth of God.' For, rightly understanding man's part, we must
make a start totally different from the anthropological preoccupation
that characterizes Tillich. There can be no thought of man in
himself knowing God even in the form of a question. That he knows
God is due to God alone and the determination in which he is
involved by the fact of God being what and who he is. 'With and
in the fact that God is ready within himself to be known by man,
man is also ready to know him.'[3] If God is the answer to man's
question, it must also be added that God is also the question itself.
'Beyond [God's] word there are no questions. All our questions arise
only as we are questioned by this last Word. . . . Even the question
that still remains can be only a question of understanding, a question
which presupposes the givenness of its answer.'[4] The existentialist
in Tillich finds in human existence, with its ultimate concern and

---

[1] *Church Dogmatics* II/1, Edinburgh 1957. The reference to Tillich is on p. 635,
where the eternity of God is discussed, and mention is made that Tillich (and Bultmann)
once 'believed that they could welcome me as one of themselves'!

[2] Op. cit. 63.   [3] Op. cit. 128.   [4] Op. cit. 154 f.

its consequent formal faith, that to which God is the answer that can ultimately sustain it. This, Barth says, is to divide into two what is one thing only. The fact that men have faith is irrelevant: 'It is not a matter of faith, but of true and certain faith. If our question is to be answered aright, an answer must be given to it which does not start from the believing man but from Jesus Christ as the object and foundation of faith.' Apart from this, 'our own reality, the enemy of grace living in us all, still remains to jeopardise the whole relationship.'[1]

What then has Barth to say positively about the relationship between God and man at this point, and what concerning the place of the faith which the business of salvation requires? He formulates the question in this way: 'How far, alongside and under Christology, is there also a Christian anthropology and ecclesiology wholly dependent of course on it and with strict reference to it? How do we come to participate in what Jesus Christ is?'[2] The easy reply, he goes on to say, is to refer to the 'possibility, necessity and reality of faith'; and he allows that this reply is correct enough so far as it goes. But it tends to obscure the situation. For what is this faith that is required? how is it to be distinguished from 'other possible forms of ineffectual and unsaving faith or unbelief or heresy or superstition'? and, above all, 'how are we actually to arrive at this faith, this faith which is no longer to be compromised by ourselves and our own enmity against grace?' The way in which these questions are formulated gives the clue to the only kind of answer possible; and it is an answer that turns its back decisively upon any kind of anthropological or existentialist suggestion. To understand this faith and what it means, we must not turn to man regarded as already having an as it were ready-made faith at his disposal to be accorded to this or that worthy or unworthy object. We have to turn to Jesus Christ. The relevant passage must be quoted at some length. 'Basically, then, the right answer can only be that as the one and only man ready for God, Jesus Christ has not only lived, died and risen for us once in time, so that the abounding grace of God might be an event and at the same time revelation among us, but as this same One he stands before his Father now in eternity for us, and lives for us in God himself as the Son of God he was and is and will be. Thus our appropriation of what he has won for us has not first to be executed by us. By the fact that he is for us in eternity in

---

[1] Op. cit. 155 f.   [2] Op. cit. 155.

F

God himself the man who is ready for God, it is executed in eternity in God himself, by him, in the eternal continuation of his high-priestly office. But this means—and what follows can only be a sequel and explanation of this proper and original truth—that Jesus Christ himself sees to it that in him and by him we are not outside but inside. He himself sees to it that his readiness is valid for us who are not identical with him, and who in ourselves are not ready for God. . . . If he is for us, this means—and in the last resort only this means—that with the eternal certainty proper to the Son of God we too are present, genuinely participating in what he is and has done.'[1]

Two remarks are called for at this point. Anticipating what will later be said, we see how powerfully Barth utilizes the conception of the representative character and function of Jesus Christ, and note that when it is so used we are within sight of the contribution which the application of the 'in Christ' can make to the whole problem. The other remark is explanatory. Barth has here been expounded in particular contrast to Tillich. In fact, this has only a methodological significance. The exposition has probably made it sufficiently clear that he stands as representative of a view opposed to that of all those who think of faith as a human possession or contribution to be offered as a condition prior to the enjoyment of salvation.

5. A matter of paradox

That attitudes so radically different and indeed opposite can be adopted in this matter is no cause for surprise. The fact is that we are faced here by a paradox.[2] In the nature of things, a paradox cannot be defined; it can only be described and analogized. The visitor to the Great Pyramid can from ground level see only one or at most two faces rising to where the eye can follow them no further; but he can also climb to the top and from the apex see all the sides at once. With paradox we remain at ground level, can only see each of the faces in turn rising convergently, and can never occupy the

---

[1] Op. cit. 156.
[2] *Pace* J. McIntyre, *The Christian Doctrine of History*, Edinburgh 1957, 97 f., where it is pointed out that in the case of the 'paradox' of freedom and grace, 'the two members of the paradox are not co-ordinates; the one conditions the other's existence and in addition limits the form which it may take, reducing the possibilities until there remains only the possibility of freedom unto faith.' This caution upon the use of the term paradox is to be accepted without reservation.

apex where the point of meeting is visible. That there is such a
meeting-place is not a matter of direct observation but the postulate
of some other kind of discernment. So in the matter of salvation,
the faith which constitutes the relation between God and man may
be described in turn from man's side as man's offering, and from
God's side as his pure gift. Brunner is aware of the paradox represented at this point by the subjective and the objective aspects of
salvation. He says:[1] 'As the Mediator, Christ, in his person and his
work is the unfathomable mystery of God, into which we cannot
and ought not to penetrate, so also the atonement in its paradoxical
combination of the subjective and the objective, of the historical
and the present, of the Word and the Spirit, is the unfathomable
mystery of God.' He goes on to say: 'We are already on false lines
. . . when we separate the thought of the fact of salvation from the
appropriation of salvation. The rubric: "appropriation of salvation"
is used frequently in dogmatics only when the conception of salvation has already been falsely materialised, and has become a rigid
orthodox doctrine.' We are certainly right to heed the warning
contained in these words. Yet of the separation against which the
caution is uttered Brunner is forced to admit that 'in the doctrinal
presentation of the subject it can scarcely be avoided'.

The negative reason is no less powerful. A paradox involves a
nice balance which is difficult to maintain. That it has not always
been maintained is demonstrated by the course of Christian doctrine.
H. A. A. Kennedy finds[2] traces of failure in St Paul himself: 'When
he speaks of God justifying a man because of his faith, receiving him
into a new relation, the relation of a child to his Father, his language
seems at times unduly to objectify the process, to keep it apart from
the experience of the individual.' And Gore has said[3] that the
tendency to isolate the thought 'Christ for us' from the other
thought 'Christ in us' has been historically 'an abundant source of
scandal'. Illustration of this is readily found in the different judgments that have been passed upon the celebrated doctrine expounded
in Anselm's *Cur Deus Homo?* To this doctrine, Denney pays the

[1] *The Mediator*, 528. Cf. *per contra* I. T. Ramsey (*Freedom and Immortality*, London
1960, 59) who seems to dismiss the problem of freedom and grace too lightly as a 'pseudo-
problem which disappears when the appropriate logical placings are given to each
phrase'. What he says has the appearance of logical jugglery, though it is by no means
unhelpful. We must, however, say something—*non ut diceretur*, as St Augustine said,
sed ne taceretur.
[2] *The Theology of the Epistles*, London 1919, 124.
[3] *Belief in Christ*, London 1921, 299.

tribute that it is 'the truest and greatest book on the atonement that has ever been written'. But Harnack's appreciation is that 'no theory so bad had ever before his day been given out as ecclesiastical'; and G. B. Stevens has said of it that 'it would be difficult to name any prominent treatise on atonement, whose conception of sin is so essentially unethical and superficial.'[1] How does it come about that so great a variety of judgments can be passed upon a single work? The reason is clear. Regarded critically, Anselm's conception of the atonement may be said to deal faithfully with the objective or divine side, with what has happened to make salvation *possible*, but it is defective upon the subjective side in explaining how this possible salvation is made *ours*. In the last resort, the impression given is of a transaction carried out between God and the God-Man at the most exalted level; but the complementary aspect requisite to a balanced understanding of the atonement, the application of this sublime transaction to men, receives insufficient notice. In other words, the precarious balance has not been maintained. Denney, with his reiterated emphasis on the atonement being 'outside of us' and a 'finished work in which God in Christ makes a final revelation of himself in relation to sinners and sin',[2] naturally finds no kind of offence in such a conception. Harnack, on the other hand, and no less characteristically, lays emphasis on the responsive side which must be ethically and not merely forensically effected, and consequently regards Anselm's doctrine as seriously defective. Stevens, similarly emphasizing the need to understand whatever is done in Christ's work for us in ethical terms, can only conclude that Anselm's view is unethical.

We thus find a recurrent tendency to emphasize one side to the detriment of the other, even where the presence of paradox is not unsuspected. It is certainly a bold venture to attempt an exposition which will maintain the required balance where so many in the long course of Christian theology, we will not say have failed to maintain it, but rather have failed to convince their readers that they have succeeded. Yet one is obliged to do what he can in difficult matters as well as in simple.

[1] The citations are given in J. K. Mozley, *The Doctrine of the Atonement*, London 1915 ff. The references are in turn from: *The Atonement and the Modern Mind*, London 1903, 116; *The History of Dogma*, Eng. trs., 1893–9, vol. VI, 78; *The Christian Doctrine of Salvation*, Edinburgh 1905, 242.
[2] *The Atonement and the Modern Mind*, 99.

6. *Obedience as solution*

Tua res agitur—how is the business done made ours? The answer in terms merely of faith has proved equivocal. A fresh approach can, however, be made if the question be formulated differently. Let us put it in this form: how are we related to Christ so that what *he* does for us is done for *us*? Three distinguishable principles have been used to answer this question: obedience, imitation, and participation, and we look at each in turn.

From a phase of Christian thought which is now almost past, there has come down to us the familiar phrase 'the life and teaching of Jesus'. It is a phrase that 'caught on' when liberalism dominated theological thought, and, even if it does not commend itself so warmly or so widely to theologians today, it governs the thought of many Christians who make no theological pretensions. Besides, some of the works written under its influence are of lasting value,[1] and have much to say perhaps especially to theologians.

When the teaching of Jesus is held to be the governing principle of the Christian life, obedience is the form in which the relation between him and his people is construed. It was only natural that with the rediscovery of the historical Jesus this element in the New Testament witness should come to be emphasized afresh. Our Lord spent much of his time in this way: 'Jesus went about teaching' (Matt. 4.23; 9.35; Luke 13.10; and cf. Matt. 21.23; 23.55; 28.20; Luke 23.5). The element of *didache* has in recent years been elevated again into a position of fundamental importance in the witness of the early Church. Further, the Gospels are largely constituted, not by the narrative of incidents, but by the record of dominical words (cf. the solid blocks of teaching recorded, e.g. Matt. 24 and 25; John 13–17). Above all, there is the Sermon on the Mount, which for unreflective Christians is the sum and substance of Christianity. However, acceptance of the idea that the role of Jesus is primarily that of teacher, and that of ourselves of obedience, raises more problems than are usually recognized. In particular, the 'Be ye therefore perfect, even as your Father which is in heaven is perfect' (Matt. 5.48) arouses perplexity in even the least reflective. This sense of perplexity was isolated, expressed and justified by

[1] The present writer owes debts to, for example, J. S. Stewart, *The Life and Teaching of Jesus Christ*, London 1933, and W. A. Curtis, *Jesus Christ the Teacher*, Oxford 1943.

R. Niebuhr[1] under the rubric 'the relevance of an impossible ideal'. It was all too plain: the Sermon on the Mount demanded the impossible, though in some sense it was held none the less to be relevant. But once the matter has been formulated in this way, it was necessary to determine what the nature of its relevance is. Is the Sermon a code of ethics? Its apparent impossibility could then be understood, for we have learned from Kant if from no other teacher that the categorical peremptoriness of the ethical imperative is quite independent of men's compliance with it in even a single instance. What the Sermon then gives us is no more than a new though better law. But, if St Paul rightly interprets our Lord, what Christ does was by his own fulfilment of the law to set us free from it. Again, it has to be pointed out that, if the Sermon is a new code of ethics, then it is applicable to all; for certainly it can hardly be doubted that no more sublime formulation of ethical principles has ever been composed. But does it in fact apply to all? —even to those who do no more than read the Sermon and try to obey it, without taking into account him who utters it? The question can hardly be answered except in the negative. The Sermon is not so much a code of ethics as a description of the way of life of certain people only. Who these certain people are is just as clear: they are Jesus' disciples, not those who merely hear what he says and try to do it, but those rather who are his followers. But if so, the basis of the Christian life lies elsewhere than in the mere acceptance of the teaching, and of course at a much deeper level. It lies in some closer relation to him who taught.

7. Imitation as solution

Is this deeper basis to be found in the principle of imitation? When the teaching of Jesus is joined as it often is with the life of Jesus, as in the liberalistic phrase, more is involved than mere obedience of some kind to him who said it. Clearly there are scriptural indications that imitation is enjoined on those who would be Christians. 'Take my yoke upon you, and learn of me' (Matt. 11.29), says Jesus; and the frequent command to 'follow me' (Matt. 4.19 etc. and parallels), often joined with the words 'take up his cross' (Matt. 16.24 and parallels), reiterated by St Paul: 'Be ye followers of me, even as I also am of Christ' (I Cor. 11.1 etc.), certainly

[1] *An Interpretation of Christian Ethics*, London 1936, ch. 4.

carries with it the injunction of imitation, besides that of bare accompaniment. Jesus is to be taken as example: 'I have given you an example' (John 13.15).

But it is evident that the injunction to imitate can operate only under restrictions. For one thing, the same difficulty as was apparent in the case of the Sermon on the Mount understood as a new and better code of conduct recurs here in another form. Examples are no doubt useful and salutary; but it is no less possible for them to be discouraging rather than encouraging. When the exemplar is manifestly far superior in accomplishment to what those who imitate can hope to achieve, the effect is depressing. The distance separating the model that is offered and the copy that is possible is too great. Then the last state is, if not worse than the first, at least little better.

It is true that Abelard, who may be regarded as the most outstanding exponent of the kind of view being considered, shows himself aware of the need to furnish more than mere example. Accordingly he supplies what amounts to a motive force. 'The manifestation of God's love to us in Christ awakens an answering love in us';[1] and again: the death of Christ is 'a revelation of the love of God, intended to call forth answering love in man', for 'gratitude is the last spark of the divine image to disappear from the soul of man'.[2] There is, however, a precondition which must be fulfilled before this answering love and gratitude can be evoked in us and so released to supply the motive power. It is that there really is something discernible for which we may be grateful and which can then provoke us to love; and this something must be more than merely an example offered to us. Denney puts it pungently[3] when he says that I cannot be expected to be grateful simply because, when drowning myself, someone else throws himself into the water to be with me; for the situation is changed only in that instead of one drowning man there are now two. A man must see that what is being done is for him and benefits him; otherwise the motive force of gratitude lies dormant and unemployable. But this crucial factor is never supplied by those who conceive the Christian life in terms of imitation. The heart of the matter has still to be discovered and defined.

But the principle of imitation is limited by another and more

---

[1] R. S. Franks, *A History of the Doctrine of the Work of Christ*, London 1918, I, 189.
[2] H. Rashdall, *The Idea of Atonement in Christian Theology*, London 1920, 360 f.
[3] I have not been able to locate the exact reference.

serious consideration. There are points at which we may and must follow the rule of the *imitatio Christi*; but just as clearly there are points where we may not and cannot. Passages have already been cited in which Christians are dominically enjoined to imitate our Lord. Certainly these words are not said meaninglessly. On the contrary, one is privileged to know in them the closeness with which our Lord was pleased to draw to himself those whom he did not disdain to call his friends (John 15.14 f.) and his brethren (Matt. 12.48; Mark 3.34). But there are passages of a quite different character, which, so far from expressing his community with them, emphasize the distance between himself and other men. 'The Son of man is come to seek and to save that which was lost' (Luke 19.10) —in this we cannot follow him. 'The Son of man came to give his life a ransom for many' (Matt. 20.28; Mark 10.45)—this we cannot do in imitation of him. 'My God, my God, why hast thou forsaken me?' (Matt. 27.46; Mark 15.34)—and, although the Psalmist too uses the words (Ps. 22.1), no one will say that the Christian is enjoined to be where Jesus Christ was when they were said by him. To set the matter in a wider context: in Gen. 22.1 ff., Abraham is ready to offer up his own son. However, his confidence that *Deus providebit* is literally justified: he is spared this supreme sacrifice. But this indulgence God does not permit himself: finally he does not spare his own Son but offers him up for us all (Rom. 8.32).[1]

The principle of imitation, then, carries us only part of the way, and indeed only a small part. For the fact is that Jesus Christ does things which, precisely because he does them, we do not ourselves need to do, and imitation can carry us at such points no further. Moreover, only because he does them is imitation at other points possible for us at all.

It is not possible to save the position by the suggestion that imitation relates us to what is human in Jesus Christ and its application stops short only of that which is divine in him. At the cross, there is only one death. Jesus Christ does not die two deaths, one as example for all to follow, and the other to effect some divine purpose and end. The purpose is one and the death is one. At this crucial point, the principle of imitation leaves us with nothing more than the injunction to realize in our lives some wan representation and reflection of the spirit which in Christ's case led him to Golgotha. In other words, the principle of imitation promises much, but

[1] See Karl Barth, *Kirchliche Dogmatik* III/3 40 f. (Eng. trs. 35).

finally fails to fulfil the promise. It seems to effect a close though external relation between men and Christ and to establish as well as enjoin a resemblance between them. The resemblance was indeed proposed at a level which can only be regarded as superficial. And it turns out that the profundities cannot thus be concealed. The chasm between the Christian and the Christ is not to be bridged in this manner; and the sign of this impossibility is the recognition of those aspects in which imitation of Christ is neither asked nor possible.[1]

8. *Participation as solution*

The third principle in whose light the Christian life can be represented is that of participation. The passage to it has been partly made in the discovery of the inadequacy of the principle of imitation. Participation enables us to do justice to that certain difference which distinguishes Christ from those who benefit from what he does. No one expresses this distinction better than James Denney:[2] 'Christ died for our sins. *That death* we do not die.' P. T. Forsyth also apprehended the importance of the distinction and expressed it even more succinctly:[3] 'He saved us by his difference from us'; and St Augustine says:[4] '*Christus de te sibi habebat carnem, de se tibi salutem; de te sibi mortem, de se tibi vitam; de te sibi contumelias, de se tibi honores.*' This is to take the *pro nobis* in all seriousness. The representation is clear. Christ is in such a way other than we are that he is able to do for us what we could not and cannot do for ourselves, and we are in consequence beneficiaries of his work. Yet of course, if we are effectually to be made beneficiaries, it is not enough to say merely that he is other. If indeed what was done were similar to the repayment of a debt, it would suffice to say that Christ wins our discharge, for, however the repayment is made, the debt is thereby cancelled and the debtor acquitted. But this would be to fall back into modes of thought suggested by Anselm and to become vulnerable to the criticism of an insufficiently serious ethical interest. The matter is otherwise stated by those who employ the principle of participation. The otherness which Christ displays

---

[1] St Francis expressed a realization of this when, as we are told, he fasted for forty days, but, lest he should seem to emulate his Lord too closely, took half a loaf of bread with him.

[2] *Studies in Theology*, London 1894, 126; cf. *The Death of Christ*, London 1902, 237: 'Christ does not commit sin, and we do not make atonement.'

[3] *The Cruciality of the Cross*, London 1909, 85.   [4] *Enarr. in Ps.* 60.3.

in his work is construed as that of representative or of substitute. Forsyth, for example, prefers the first term. To the words already quoted he adds: 'He did not redeem us because he represented us; rather he represents us because he redeemed us.' Denney on the other hand prefers the second term:[1] 'A representative not produced by us, but given to us—not chosen by us, but elect of God—is not a representative at all, but a substitute. [Christ accordingly] stands in our stead'; and he quotes the line of the well-known hymn: 'In my place condemned he stood.' The difference is important. No doubt Denney prepares the case he opposes in a way which makes it easy to demolish: if a representative can only be chosen by those he represents, then clearly the term does not apply to Christ. But the case is not settled by this narrow definition. In the New Testament, the idea is certainly apparent. In Rom. 5.12 ff. and I Cor. 15.22, it is supported by the analogy of Adam in whom we all die; and whatever we make of this analogy, it is cavalier to speak, as Denney does, of 'the fantastic abstraction of a "racial act" which is the atonement in the sense of the New Testament'. On the other hand, the New Testament support for the idea of substitute is perhaps not any easier to understand intellectually. It has to fall back upon the concept of sacrifice and the sacrificial victim. But everyone knows that no unanimous answer has been found for the question how or why exactly sacrifice effects anything. Hence on either view of the way in which the otherness of Christ is interpreted, we are left with at least an intellectual difficulty on our hands. This in turn implies that neither of the terms, representative or substitute, is automatically the key for understanding how it comes about that what is done by Jesus Christ is made ours.

Can we press any further into what must finally remain mysterious by means of the idea of participation? The attempt may be made by looking more closely at the benefits in which we are said to participate. In some of these we may be said to participate under a rule of contrariety, and in others under a rule of correspondence. On the one hand, as has been already said, men participate in benefits acquired for them by Jesus Christ, and by his work and grace they are admitted to possession of what otherwise could never be theirs. In general, these benefits may be summed up in such terms as forgiveness, or reconciliation, or simply salvation. Here is where the rule of contrariety operates: Christ wins

[1] *The Atonement and the Modern Mind*, 99.

these benefits for us who had himself no need of them and has himself no part in them. The New Testament is full of references to such benefits. Because he died, we live; because he suffered, we rejoice; because he was reckoned guilty, we are reckoned innocent; because he suffered punishment, we enjoy forgiveness; because he was condemned, we are acquitted. Of these, the principle of participation takes adequate account.

But there are other benefits in which our participation is subject to a quite different rule of correspondence: he confers some things upon us which he himself may be said to enjoy. Thus because he lives, we shall live also; because he conquers, we too are in all things conquerors; because he reigns, we shall reign with him; and so on. How can the idea of participation be extended to include these? It would not be true to say that when we think of Christ as substitute or representative, we are entirely precluded from reckoning with these benefits which both Christ and we may be said to enjoy. But this reckoning will have to be in the nature of an afterthought. To the benefits which we enjoy because Christ is *pro nobis*, we should have to add as supplement those which we enjoy because Christ is also *in nobis*. In other words, we should attribute to the incarnate and crucified Christ the benefits of which he himself has no need, and we should attribute to the risen, exalted and regnant Christ those blessings which he enjoys with us. That this is a satisfactory solution can hardly be allowed. For would not Christ then be divided? Should we not be saying that we derive some of the benefits we enjoy from one Christ and the rest from another? Should we not then be looking to the historical events of Christ's career including both his life and his death to supply one part of the basis for the Christian life, and then have to turn for the other part to an eternal Christ? This would certainly be to incur grave theological risks.

9. *In Christ*

It does not, however, appear that the principle of participation necessarily involves them. Hitherto participation has been expounded in the sense that it is benefits which are shared. The difficulty implicit in adopting this sense is that Christ is separated from the benefits which he has acquired and offers, and our participation in these benefits becomes thus loosed from our relation to him. This is the root cause of the difficulty that then arises in knowing how to represent to ourselves the way in which what he has acquired can become ours; and this in turn is simply another form of a difficulty which has already been considered, how acceptance of these proffered benefits is possible for us. Must not the solution lie in our having a closer relation to him who offers them? For the question: in what do we participate in being Christians? allows of another answer. It may be answered in terms already used: the Christian is one who is in Christ. As has been said, Barth poses the question:[1] 'How do we come to participate in what Jesus Christ is?' The form of the question is at least correct: the participation which makes men Christian is not primarily in benefits which Christ holds out to them apart from himself; it is rather in him who holds them out. Then as consequence what he holds and all that he holds become ours.[2] In other words, that Christ is *pro nobis* and also *in nobis* has to be supplemented by and understood in terms of the *nos in Christo*.

Implicitly, though not perhaps very often explicitly, this has frequently been said. Brunner has this to say:[3] 'It is only in this subjective experience, in faith, that the atonement becomes real. But this subjective experience is completely objective in character. For this is what it means: my "self" is crossed out, displaced, and replaced by Christ, the Divine Word.' He goes on to point out that others have said the same thing in different words. Luther talks of a *'fröhliche Wirtschaft'*, a happy exchange, by which Christ becomes mine and I become his: *'Nostra assumsit, ut nobis sua conferret.'* Irenaeus, in a well-known phrase, has this to say: 'For the sake of his infinite love he has become what we are, in order that he may make us entirely what he is';[4] and from the *Epistle to Diognetus* 9 comes the statement: 'God gave his own Son for us as a ransom, the holy for the unholy, . . . the imperishable for the perishing. . . . O marvellous exchange, O incomprehensible work!' Brunner comments: this 'in a variety of forms is the main theme of the Christian message of the early Church'.

In Christ—methodologically we may distinguish an objective and a subjective use of the phrase. Objectively it means that Christ does

---

[1] *Kirchliche Dogmatik* II/1 173 (Eng. trs. 155).
[2] See T. F. Torrance, *The School of Faith*, cx: 'It is through partaking of Christ himself that we partake of his benefits and blessings. . . . For unless he gives himself to us first, his blessings are not ours.'
[3] *The Mediator*, 524 f.   [4] *Haer.* V, preface.

a work by which we infinitely benefit. It is a work finished and complete and which requires no supplement or addition from any quarter. A new humanity is offered to man to replace fallen humanity. This is the Christ *pro nobis*. If the matter were left there, we should still have to think in terms of acceptance of the offer by the men whom it is meant to benefit; and the old problem of what Christ does and what we do to make effective or at least applicable what he does would break out afresh. But the matter does not conclude there. He who makes the offer has himself assumed humanity. In the incarnation, Christ became what he offered. Further, he became it for us, in such a sense that we must not only say 'God was in Christ' but also we are in Christ. The existentialist theologians are right when they say that we find our 'authentic being' in Christ. But they are wrong in representing this as the achievement of an independent and deliberate choice which they impose as a burden on those who are to become Christians. We find our 'authentic being' in Christ in that we are what he is, and this we become because by his person and work he makes us so.

It is true that by involving us in this conclusion the argument has not told us how we ought to understand what man's part in salvation is. The question raised at the beginning of this chapter concerning the meaning of our 'need only to accept what has already been made available' for us has not been answered; it has been by-passed. This will have to be given consideration in the chapter which follows. Here we must simply recognize the fact that Christianity proposes and offers a new mode of being. The Christian's relation to Christ is not properly described in terms of mysticism. For mysticism entails the final relinquishment of individuality. It may indeed be described as a kind of *ekstasis*, as Brunner remarks;[1] but it is so in quite a different manner from that proposed by mysticism. For the ecstasy of mysticism is a subjective experience, while the ecstasy of the Christian's relation to Christ is 'independent of all subjective experiences. It means that one is placed at a point outside the stream of experience, on the further bank, which therefore cannot be touched by the stream of experience any more, because where I stand is not the position *I* have chosen; it is not my doing, but has been chosen by God, because it is God's act, in an objective fact, because it is the cross of Christ.' The Christian's relation to Christ is not properly described in separatist terms. This on the whole

[1] *The Mediator*, 526.

was the fault of Orthodoxy. It conceived of Christ's beneficiary and
the Christian's benefactor as separated from one another, and could
then never effectively span the gulf which it dug between them.
Nor is the relation properly construed in the more modern terms
which a philosophy of personalism has more recently been pro-
posing. Despite all that is to be learned from Buber's concept of the
I-Thou—and certainly it does bring us nearer the truth of man's
dealings with God and God's with man—we must judge it to be
applicable rather to the mode in which these dealings are carried
on, but to be unable to help us much concerning the means by which
they are made possible. The 'in Christ' posits a unique relation,
one which is prepared for us and into which we have been taken.
Then indeed we find our true and authentic self, but we do so as
we discover that we have been taken by another and are thus
grounded in him.

10. *One body in Christ*

A further implication should be noted. Given its proper value in
the Christian scheme of things, the 'in Christ' shifts the centre of
gravity from what must be done in order that we be saved to what
has been done for this end. By the same token, it shifts the centre
of gravity from the individual to the Church.

St Paul often speaks in highly individualistic singular terms, and
his more characteristic 'we' is frequently individuated into 'I' and
'you'. This happens when he writes autobiographically (Gal. 1
and 2), or speaks of the initiation of his career as a Christian (e.g.
I Cor. 15.8). But in the most important of these passages his terms
lead him to the concept not of 'I in Christ' but of 'Christ in me'
(Gal. 2.20). Often too St Paul's 'I' is clearly representative and does
duty for others besides himself (e.g. Rom. 7.7-25);[1] and with this
may be compared II Cor. 5.16 where the representative relation is
looked at from the other end and a 'we' is used when it is not certain
that St Paul can be included in the number. In general, St Paul
powerfully emphasizes his own solidarity with other Christians
and theirs with him. When he refers to Christians as those who are
in Christ, he is thinking in corporate terms: the term 'members'

---

[1] See especially v. 14, where 'we' makes a sudden appearance, but only, it seems, to
emphasize a distinction between the I that knows and the I that is carnally disabled
from action in accordance with this knowledge.

takes the place of individuals, and 'body' represents the solidarity in which they stand. There is 'one body in Christ' (Rom. 12.5).

Two recent studies in English have expressed the two typical attitudes that are possible here. J. A. T. Robinson says[1] that 'the concept of the body supplies the lynch-pin of Paul's thought. For we are here at the very pivotal point on which the whole of his theology turns, and by virtue of which also it is distinctive in the New Testament.' With this judgment E. Best[2] would probably agree. There is a further area of agreement: the ideas of the body of Christ and of the Church stand in the closest relation to one another. Best says:[3] 'The body of Christ is in some way Christ himself and the members of his body are in some way his members'; and Robinson speaks[4] of 'the inextricable relatedness of all Paul's uses of *sōma*', and of the 'success of his description of the Church as the body of Christ'. When the nature of the relation is more closely defined, however, difference becomes apparent. 'Christians,' says Robinson,[5] 'form Christ's body . . . they are in literal fact the risen organism of Christ's person in all its concrete reality. What is arresting is [Paul's] identification of this personality with the Church.' On the other hand, this is denied by Best who not only says[6] that 'Paul wishes to evade the identification of Christ and the Church', but even more strongly declares[7] that 'the Church is not really and ontologically the body of Christ' but only 'metaphorically'.[8] But at all events both affirm the truth that on the biblical view the Christian is never thought of as an isolated and individual believer but always as a member of the Church.[9] In being a Christian he is member of what St Paul calls the body of Christ.

What implications follow from this truth? Does the fact that Christian and body of Christ are necessarily related throw any light upon the question what it is that is the proper recipient of the life in Christ, the question how this life in Christ is imparted? Here the differences into which the general agreement bifurcates in the case of the two typical writers mentioned may be of importance. If the body of Christ is identified with the Church, then it is the Church

---

[1] *The Body*, London 1952, 48.   [2] *One Body in Christ*, London 1955.
[3] Op. cit. 111.   [4] Robinson, op. cit. 49.   [5] Op. cit. 51.
[6] Best, op. cit. 111. He admits (195), however, that 'there is a strand of thought in Paul which tends to identify Christ with the Church'.
[7] Op. cit. 100; et sim. 105.   [8] Op. cit. 112; et sim. 195.
[9] See op. cit. 190: 'It is impossible to conceive of a Christian who is not a member of the Church, which is related to Christ as in him and as his body. . . . Individual Christians consequently do not exist.'

that is the prime recipient of and participant in the life of Christ. But to be accurate we must say more than that the Church is the place where Christ imparts and makes available the life that is his; rather it is the place where Christ enjoys the life that is his. Hence there can be no thought of the individual enjoying this life on his own; and on the other hand there can be no doubt that the man who is a member of the Church (in any sense that may be subsequently defined) has imparted to him the life which belongs to the body of Christ. The body is the bearer of the life which Christ both has and imparts.[1] The identification of body and Christ involves a primacy of the body or Church over the individual, and this in turn involves the deliberate rejection of any suggestion that the life of the body or Church is constituted by whatever individuals can bring or contribute.[2] 'Know ye not that your bodies are the members of Christ?' asks St Paul (I Cor. 6.15). This Robinson regards[3] as a clear reference 'not to a society but to a person, viz. Christ', and its meaning is 'that individuals are members of a person'. When *sōma* is applied to the Church it means 'something *not corporate but corporal*. It directed the mind to a person; it did not itself suggest a social group.' Hence too a bridge is built between the historical events of the Gospel and the men of today. Christ still lives among men; and if we cannot say that Christ simply is the Church, we must say that Christ's body is the Church. 'Christ is incarnate in the Church. . . . Here . . . is Christ still living and working amongst men, once in his physical body, now in his mystical body, the Church.'[4] Life is imparted to men as in the Church they become literally part of his body.

On the other hand, Best believes that the phrase 'body of Christ' is applied to the Church in a metaphorical sense only. The way in which impartation of the life takes place is in consequence differently conceived. In place of Robinson's *corporal* he prefers *corporate*.

---

[1] As Fritz Neugebauer says (*In Christus*, 99), 'the Church is both the object of God's saving activity and God's saving activity itself.'

[2] St Paul can call the Church 'the righteousness of God in Christ' (II Cor. 5.21). This can only be because the Church may be said to be righteous (in Christ, eschatologically) even while it is not righteous (in itself, empirically). But the idea of the Church in Christ and so its identification with the righteousness of God is as real as the Church that is empirically so far from being wholly righteous. The righteousness of God that the Church is is not constituted by the righteousness that the Church we empirically know displays. *A fortiori*, the Church is not constituted by the sum of its individual members.

[3] Robinson, op. cit. 50.

[4] Best, op. cit. 197—words used, it need hardly be said, to express a view which the author thinks must be rejected.

He finds[1] two fundamental ideas in the formula 'in Christ': 'believers are "in Christ"; the place of salvation is Jesus Christ (or salvation is "in Christ")'; and 'these two fundamental ideas are linked through the conception of Christ as in some way a corporate personality.' This clearly is the point at which the possible different roads divide, and this too the consideration which requires Best to regard the application of the phrase 'body of Christ' to the Church as metaphorical.

Neither view is without qualification satisfactory. Clearly Robinson overbids his hand. If it is true that 'the appearance on which Paul's whole faith and apostleship was founded was the revelation of the resurrection body of Christ, not as an individual, but as the Christian community',[2] how is his conversion to the Christian faith different from any other subsequent conversion; how could he have claimed successfully the special place accorded to him among the apostles; and what could he have meant by calling himself an *ektrōma*, 'one born out of due time' (I Cor. 15.8)? And the suggestion that a 'physical' union of the believer with Christ is implied by the use of *kollasthai* which has a sexual connotation collapses when confronted with the use at Rom. 12.9 of the same word in a context that makes physical union or anything like it impossible.[3] On the other hand, it is difficult to be content to call St Paul's use of the body of Christ in application to the Church merely metaphorical unless the kind of metaphor is more closely defined.[4]

In fact both writers resile from the extreme positions which in their more intransigent moments they seem about to occupy. At some points in his exposition, Robinson is quite content not to press the identity he elsewhere suggests and supports. There is in St Paul's use of the word 'body', if not ambiguity, at least comprehensiveness: there are 'two uses (one can hardly say "senses") of

---

[1] Op. cit. 21.   [2] Robinson, op. cit. 58.

[3] Robinson seems to err in at least sometimes identifying the Church as the body of Christ with the person of Christ in an absolute sense. We may rightly identify the Church with the body of Christ, but we cannot rightly say that Christ is the Church. Fritz Neugebauer (*In Christus*, 98) holds that St Paul remains true to the structure of his anthropology throughout. 'In Christ' is defined in terms of what Christ did and what happened to him: 'the Church is the body of Christ because what happened to it happened to the body of Christ.'

[4] See Robinson's comment, op. cit. 51: 'To say that the Church is the body of Christ is no more of a metaphor than to say that the flesh of the incarnate Jesus or the bread of the Eucharist is the body of Christ. None of them is "like" his body (Paul never says this); each of them *is* the body of Christ, in that each is the physical complement and extension of the one and the same Person and Life. They are all expressions of a single Christology.'

G

the word': in Rom. 7.4, the words 'through the body of Christ' 'mean *both* "through the fact that Christ in his flesh died to the law" *and* "through the fact that you now are joined to and are part of that body" '; and the Pauline Gospel depends on 'you hath he reconciled in the body of his flesh through his death' being held in the closest conjunction with Eph. 2.15: 'that he . . . might reconcile them both in one body unto God through the cross.'[1] This seems to be almost exactly what Best contends for—a many-sided employment of the expression 'body' which, along with other considerations,[2] render simple identification of the two concepts inaccurate as an interpretation of St Paul's thought.

At points, then, the difference between the two views expounded almost vanishes. Yet the main sense of the one view retains its distinctive character over against the other. The tendency to identify the body of Christ with the Church implies that it is to the Church that the life in Christ is primarily imparted; to hold that the body of Christ is only metaphorically declared to be the Church suggests that the life is primarily imparted to the individual, and that the Church is no more than, to begin with, the occasion of his individual participation in that life, and then, subsequently, the sphere in which that life has to be manifested. Either we are members of his body and so in Christ; or we are in Christ and so members of his body. The one tendency, as Best points out,[3] when pursued to its extreme, leads to the position of the Roman Church; there are some who still wish to follow the other, as Robinson hints,[4] but it can only lead them to the sectarian or gathered Church.

If there is a dilemma here, Karl Barth proposes a way out, in a typically dynamic understanding of what life in Christ really means. He conceives the being of the Christian as falling under the rubric of calling: in pregnant phrase,[5] 'it is as witness to him that he takes and installs him'. But if the Christian's calling is to witness, it is also immediately a calling into an already established community. There can be no solitary witness; there is only the task of witnessing which is already being carried out by others engaged in it. Indeed this is so from the very beginning. It is twelve men that Jesus Christ calls at the outset of his ministry, clearly intending them to be the Christian successors to the sons of Jacob. As the latter were the patriarchs of Israel, the old community and people of God, so the

---

[1] Op. cit. 47.　　　　[2] Best, op. cit. 138.　　　　[3] Op. cit. 199.
[4] Robinson, op. cit. 7.　　[5] *Kirchliche Dogmatik* IV/3 781 (Eng. trs. 682).

twelve disciples are the patriarchs of the new. One is of this society as he does what it does. The antithesis between Church and individual as the subject of life in Christ has been overcome.

The direction in which Barth's strongly actualist argument tends is surely right. No doubt entry into the Church is achieved individually, as men *singulatim* answer the *hic et nunc* summons addressed to them. But it is not they who then bring the Church into existence. On the contrary, they are received into that which is already there. The Church is not an association or corporation of like-minded individuals;[1] and its unity does not have only such strength as their like-mindedness possesses and so can confer. On the contrary, its unity rests upon what Christ has done, and is thus already complete and inviolate. It is the humanity in which all men share that is renewed by Jesus Christ (with all the ambiguity attaching to the little word *is*). Within this sphere, there is further created a body of those who simply acknowledge what has been done for them and for all men (in whose case the ambiguity of the *is* has been removed). This is what Barth says when he writes[2] that the revelation of God's love 'embraces *realiter* both the world and the community, non-Christians and Christians. But the knowledge and proclamation of it is a matter for the Christian community.' When our having been by Christ's work accorded a renewed humanity is accompanied by acknowledgment of the gift[3] and acceptance of the task, we are incorporated into the body of Christ and numbered among its members.

That this should come about in the case of any or all has origins within the purpose of God: it may not only be said that Christians are taken into the state of being in Christ, but that they are determined by God for this. But this is to be discussed in the next chapter.

[1] St Paul never speaks of a or the body of Christians or believers, but only of them as the body of Christ.

[2] *Kirchliche Dogmatik* IV/1 111 (Eng. trs. 103).

[3] Normally in baptism, in which, in the case of infants, the acknowledgment is not to be individualistically understood.

5

Determination to the Life

1. *Grace and freedom*

LIFE in Christ has its ground in Christ, his person and his work. This is the position reached at the end of the previous chapter. But the argument must be carried forward from there, if only for the reason that no secure place has yet been found in the divine scheme of salvation for the part that on all hands it is acknowledged man must somehow play. An attempt was indeed made at the beginning of the last chapter to hold this interest before us. But it was not successful. For the answer in terms of faith proved ambiguous; and when the more general question was raised, how we are related to Christ so that what he does for us becomes really ours, it was found that neither obedience nor imitation could stand as answer. We were therefore driven back on participation, only to discover that it is a participation offered independently of anything that we can do. The answer thus seemed to be that there is nothing for us to do, for it has all been done for us. Thus the course of the argument carried the attention further and further away from man's part.

The title and subject of the present chapter might seem, so far from reversing this direction of thought, to require us to move still further along the same lines. We should thus be again disabled from an intelligible understanding of what man has to do. This is not in fact the case. The attempt will be made to show that it is only when the more ultimate considerations implied in predestination are raised that it is possible to conceive the relation of God and man at this point.

At the outset indeed this attempt appears very unlikely to succeed. For when the initiative is traced back into the eternal and determining purpose of God, delicate questions concerning human freedom and responsibility and their relation to divine grace immediately raise their heads and demand answer. We are today so aware of this that it hardly needs to be said. The question of determination or predestination is transmitted to us in the course of Christian theology. We cannot evade the form which this course has imparted to it, and the terms are loaded with meaning and overtones now inseparable from them. If we could remain content with the New Testament witness, we should find the position simpler. There the outlines of the problem are stated, but without apparent awareness that there is a problem, or at least without trace of the embarrassment which it occasions in us. The elements to be taken into account are faithfully stated in the Bible; it is we who experience the perplexity.

The simplest statement of all is Phil. 2.12 f.: 'Wherefore . . . work out your own salvation with fear and trembling; for it is God which worketh in you both to do and to will of his good pleasure.' Here two factors are set down beside one another, our working out of our own salvation and God's working in us not towards a compulsive doing of his will but to an apparently inward and voluntary desire to do his will. No incongruity is apparently felt: man works, and God works; and the relation between them is not worked out. God and man are engaged; the question of man's responsibility over against God's action is not raised.

Other statements with varying reference occur but do not help very much to its clarification. The same general terms appear in Eph. 2.8 f.: 'For by grace are ye saved, through faith; and that not of yourselves: it is the gift of God: not of works, lest any man should boast.' In salvation two distinguishable factors are at work. Salvation is by grace and through faith; God and man are engaged, each with a part to play. There is some exegetical doubt about the exact reference of the words 'and that'. Three options are offered: either salvation as a whole; or the faith that has just been mentioned; or the grace incorporated in the first phrase. Not much depends on the exact reference: the meaning is in any case fairly plain. The grace here mentioned is qualified in three ways: negatively as not arising from ourselves; again negatively as not being the result of works; and positively as being simply the gift of God. On any interpretation, two factors are involved: faith which, however it arise, is not just something that we must bring with us, but which yet is really ours; and grace, purely the work of God, which apparently does not cancel or undermine what in faith we do.

Again in the case of reconciliation: 'God . . . hath reconciled us to himself by Jesus Christ'; and our consequent reconciliatory ministry is the proclamation of the fact that 'God was in Christ reconciling the world unto himself' (II Cor. 5.18 ff.). But the ministry has a hortatory corollary; God beseeches men by it: 'We pray you in Christ's stead, be ye reconciled to God.' Here again are the two factors: 'God hath reconciled' and 'be ye reconciled', without apparent recognition of incongruity. Reconciliation is not different in this regard from salvation.

With 'righteousness' we have a different term but no different treatment. Rom. 4.22 ff. raises the question of the imputation of righteousness. This imputation was effected in the case of Abraham, but it involves a principle not applicable to him alone. It applies 'for us also, to whom it shall be imputed'. But there follows immediately the conditional clause: 'if we believe on him that raised up Jesus our Lord from the dead'. Once more, two factors: where righteousness is involved, there is imputation, a clear and decisive act of God; but there is at the same time too a responsive, if not condition, at least requirement, which comes from the other side, from man: belief in God who has effected the resurrection in the case of Jesus. God imputes, but man has to believe and the imputation is for those that thus believe.

2. *The biblical statement*

The wisest course might be to let the matter go at that, and with Scripture simply to say: work yourselves, for it is God that works (Phil. 2.12 f.). For many purposes, this is in fact all that is necessary. St Paul's example is followed in the celebrated phrase that Christians are to pray as though all depended on God, and to work as though all depended on them; and the words of a familiar prayer are in the same sense: O Lord, evoke thy response in me. But the exigencies, both dogmatic and apologetic, are compelling. *Fides quaerens intellectum*—faith must understand itself and work out its implications for the double reason both of understanding itself and of being able to commend itself in intelligible form. When two factors are set beside one another in this way, the question of relation is unavoidable. If we are 'workers together with God' (II Cor. 6.1), how do the parts fit together?

When we go beyond their mere compresence, difficulties are immediately encountered. God's part, the divine factor, can or must be represented as covering the whole field. The saving of man is not only the characteristically divine work; it is also a work that only the divine can do. Further, it is not only a work that only the divine can do, but a work that the divine is manifestly competent to do. St Paul's testimony is unambiguously that 'all is of grace', and grace is God acting graciously. The dominical testimony reaffirms this. One of our Lord's simplest definitions of the end for which he came is 'to seek and to save that which is lost'; and again, the 'good shepherd' secures the safety of his sheep at the cost of his own life and without any help from the sheep. The omnicompetence of the work of God in salvation is balanced by an apparent inability in man to do anything to contribute to his salvation. Indeed the omnicompetence of God's work really excludes the possibility of a supplementary contribution from elsewhere. If man's condition is set forth in the prototype of Adam fallen, then we are those who have turned our backs upon God, and have completed the defection by setting ourselves up in God's place. If this is our case, unless God act, salvation will necessarily remain outside our grasp. The notion of a 'relic of the image of God' is not really a biblical concept; it is no more than a rationalization born of a certain interpretation of what the Bible says. The Bible contains nothing concerning a residuary spark of the divine, though such a concept is often used to make sense of the facts which the Bible records. Moreover, the biblical avoidance of the idea is corroborated by the history of the events; for at the cross, as the decisive phase of the saving work proceeds, the Son of man stands quite alone: 'they all forsook him, and fled' (Mark 14.50).[1]

But the biblical witness is not so simple as this. There runs through it an apparently contrasting strand. The Gospels record a reiterated demand on the part of our Lord for faith. Positively, 'thy faith hath saved thee' (Luke 7.50); and negatively: 'and he did not many mighty works there because of their unbelief' (Matt. 13.58). Even more emphatically, this note is sounded in the early history of the Church as recorded in the Acts: when the question is asked what has to be done for salvation, St Paul answers: 'Believe

[1] If Judas Iscariot was venerated by the Gnostic sect of the Cainites, it is a tribute not to anything in Judas, but no doubt to the omnicompetence of the work of the Saviour in bringing about whose death he had a major part to play. But the situation is complicated by the sect's advocacy of general disobedience to the Old Testament law in order to vindicate 'the Father of All' (see e.g. R. M. Grant, *Gnosticism and Early Christianity*, London, 1960, 95, 200), and by its reported possession of an apocryphal Gospel of Judas Iscariot.

on the Lord Jesus Christ, and thou shalt be saved' (Acts 16.31). And these quotations are typical of many others. Nor can we very well say that there is here simply juxtaposition of a divine and a human part. The suggestion seems to be made that man's part is the condition upon which God's part is effective. It looks in other words as if we had to make an independent contribution and bring it with us, and as if only then the matter can reach completion. Jesus waits upon faith before he does his mighty works; salvation waits upon belief before realizing itself. We are tempted then to make this division of things: the mighty work of salvation is in some limited sense a completed thing to be attributed to God; but its realization is possible only where what has been done is met by a correlative response on man's part.

But it is impossible to rest content with this easy division of labour. At crucial points, Scripture itself drastically qualifies the independence apparently won for man's part. Faith itself is represented not as a thing independent of God at all. It is indeed something that men declare and profess; but that they do declare and profess it is something that God does in them. Thus St Paul, warning the Corinthians against a certain type of apostasy *de convenance*, a temporary repudiation of Jesus Christ as Lord, when persecution makes fidelity costly, denies that it is a legitimate action; nor may anyone plead that he was given it to speak thus by the Spirit, for 'no man speaking by the Spirit of God calleth Jesus accursed'; and he continues: 'No man can say that Jesus is the Lord but by the Holy Ghost.' He comforts those who are thus hard pressed and sorely tempted: your faith will stand the day, he says, precisely because it is not something which you yourself have contrived, but something rather that has been contrived in you by the Holy Spirit (I Cor. 12.3). In the matter of faith too, God is at work. Your faith is not yours, but strictly speaking God's. Similarly also in the Gospels, the passage Matt. 16.16 ff. leaves no uncertainty: the faith confessed by St Peter is immediately detached by our Lord from its human conditions. Not all the wit or wisdom of flesh and blood enables the confession to be made; it is the work of 'my Father which is in heaven'. St Peter's faith is not St Peter's pure and simple, but at least the work of God in St Peter.

Similar conclusions have to be drawn from St Paul's use of the term 'gift'. 'It is the gift of God', he says (Eph. 2.8). It can be and has been held that this is a clear and intelligible statement of the relation of God's part to man's. 'When in the mystery of personal freedom, a man does choose rightly, what he has done is to allow divine grace to operate within him. . . . God is not able (without retracting his gift of freedom) to cause a man to choose rightly, although, when he does so choose, his choice is at once taken up into and is inextricably interpenetrated by the prevenient divine activity.'[1] But clearly this will not do, and the necessary retort is evident. 'The only prevenience here ascribed to God is that he offers his grace prior to man's allowing him to exercise it, and . . . that is not good enough.' This would be simply the familiar situation of being offered a good thing by somebody and independently deciding to accept it. But such terms as these cannot define the relations of grace and freedom. 'We must surely say not only that God graciously offers us his salvation, but also that only by his grace are we enabled to respond to it. The Christian name for this response is faith, and faith also is "the gift of God".' But this is only once again to state the old problem: God does all, and we have our part to play. Within the area covered by the action of God, men supply the element of faith; and this faith is men's response and at the same time God's gift. The problem of divine determination and human freedom is no nearer solution.

3. The traditional statement: Tertullian, St Augustine and Luther

How is it that in the scriptural witness there appears no trace of the embarrassment which affects us when we reflect upon it? It has already been suggested that the problem comes to us loaded with the consequences of prolonged theological consideration. How have these consequences affected the problem and the way in which it now presents itself today? The summary answer seems to be that, while St Paul is content to affirm that man *does not* contribute to his own salvation, the traditional orthodox affirmation has come to be that man *cannot* do so. In other words, an ontological ground has been supplied for St Paul's theological and religious insight. The provision of this ontological ground has profoundly altered the problem and the meaning of the terms in which it is stated.

For the beginning of this development, we must turn to Tertullian

---

[1] This quotation is taken from J. H. Hick, 'The Christology of D. M. Baillie', *Scottish Journal of Theology*, XI 1, March 1958, 9; the two that follow are from John Baillie: 'Some Comments on Professor Hick's Article on "The Christology of D. M. Baillie" '. *SJT* XI 3, September 1958, 269.

and the way in which he conceived grace. N. P. Williams[1] suggests that there are three senses in which Tertullian uses the term *gratia*. (*a*) There is first the sense apparent in St Paul, 'God's kindness as shown in his pardon of sins', exemplified in the phrase the 'grace of justification'. (*b*) Secondly, grace is used to designate the total spiritual effect of baptism, including pardon for past sins and the bestowal of the gift of the Holy Spirit. (*c*) Thirdly, grace is equated with a 'divine energy which works in the individual Christian, and may even override his free-will'. This last use is illustrated by Tertullian's own words: 'Even stones will become children of Abraham, if they are shaped into conformity with Abraham's faith; and even the offspring of vipers will bring forth fruits of repentance, if they first spew forth the venom of wickedness. Such will be the power of divine grace, which is assuredly mightier than nature, having in subjection to itself within us the faculty of free will.'[2] Of this understanding of grace, there is not a trace in Pauline thought. For clearly it is one thing to think of the Gospel of Christ as 'the power of God unto salvation' (Rom. 1.16) and of 'the exceeding greatness of his power to us-ward who believe' (Eph. 1.19), and quite another to think of grace itself as a sanctifying power 'detached from the idea of the personal Spirit of God, and hypostatised into an impersonal force'.[3]

Moreover, there is another correlate development to be detected in Tertullian. While on the one hand grace becomes transmuted into an external force, the subjects to whom this grace is extended are on the other hand characterized by an ineluctable *vitium originalis* or original sin. *Tradux animae, tradux peccati*—'all human nature became corrupt in the original father of the race and inherits a bias to evil',[4] thus acquiring an *alia natura*.[5] This constitutes an inherent inability in man to make any contribution to his own salvation.

This combination of human inability and grace understood as an impersonal force carries important consequences. For the first time the question of the place of man's free will over against this divine force is raised. This is to give quite a different complexion to an ancient problem. 'From now onwards the patristic opposition between "nature" and "grace" tends to push the Pauline opposition

---

[1] *The Grace of God*, 16.   [2] *De anima* 21.   [3] *The Grace of God*, 17.
[4] J. F. Bethune-Baker, *An Introduction to the Early History of Christian Doctrine*, London 1903, 8th ed. with addenda, 1949, 303.   [5] *De anima* 41.

between "works" and "grace" more and more into the background of Christian thought.'[1] In words already used, man is regarded now not merely as not contributing anything to his salvation but as being incapable of doing so. Hypostatization has thus taken place on both sides. On the side of God, grace has been loosed from the personal exercise of it by a gracious God, and denuded of the characteristic Pauline meaning of divine favour; on the side of man, the ravages of sin are regarded as so impairing him that he is now by nature unable to supply the faith which is requisite and which must therefore, in the purest sense, be a sheer gift from elsewhere. If this stops a little short of a hypostatization of evil, it should be remembered that Tertullian was not averse to admitting that demons exercise a harmful influence upon man,[2] even if this does not exempt him from responsibility and culpability. In these terms, the problem of relating the action of God to the action of men so as to preserve human freedom becomes virtually insoluble.

Yet Tertullian was laying down the lines along which Christian thought was steadily to move. St Augustine has no hesitation in affirming 'the absolute dominion of God over and in the wills of those whom he chooses to elect, whether to faith only, or to faith, final perseverance and glory'.[3] This dominion is exercised in an exterior manner by the providential arrangement of the circumstances influencing human choice. Thus: 'O Pharisee, thou that lovest little because thou thinkest that little has been forgiven thee . . . "What then," says he, "I who have never committed murder, am I to be punished for murder? I who have never committed adultery, am I to be punished for adultery?" But this says thy God unto thee: "I was guiding thee for myself, I was keeping thee for myself. That thou shouldest not commit adultery, a tempter was absent: that a tempter should be absent, I brought it about. Place and time were lacking; and that these should be lacking, I brought it about. Suppose, on the contrary, that the tempter was there, and place and time were not wanting; that thou shouldest not consent, I terrified thee. Acknowledge therefore the grace of him to whom thou owest that thou didst not commit this crime." '[4] But the dominion is apparent also interiorly: 'Who will be guilty of such impious folly as to assert that God cannot convert to the good such evil wills of men as he wishes, when he wishes, and where

[1] *The Grace of God* 17.
[3] *The Grace of God* 26.
[2] *De anima* 39.
[4] St Augustine, *Serm.* 99.6.

he wishes?"[1] Even more illuminating is the statement he elsewhere makes:[2] 'God has men's wills more in his own power than they themselves have their wills in their own power.' Here the very essence of the conception is made apparent. There is no distinction of mode between God's action upon the wills of men and their own; on the contrary, the two are distinguished upon a merely comparative basis.[3] Nothing could more clearly show the *impasse* consequent upon the hypostatization mentioned—man and God thrust apart as distinct factors, the one alone able to direct the will to good, the other totally unable. That other passages can be cited from St Augustine which tend in quite a different sense is of course true. But the implication to be drawn from this is not that the problem has been solved, but only that the two sides which constitute it receive separate mention; and the lack of system characteristic of St Augustine's writings does not admit of them being so drawn together that a solution is either possible or seen to be necessary.

Nor does Luther fare better. He makes no new start but only freshly emphasizes points already apparent in St Augustine's thought. The disastrous consequences of the fall are now represented as reaching to every part of man's nature. So ruinous are they that on occasion, as N. P. Williams points out,[4] man and sin are really identified. 'It is the essence of man to sin'; 'man, as he is born of father and mother, is with his whole nature and essence not merely a sinner but sin itself.'[5] The hypostatization of man's sinful state is now virtually complete. The result is the denial by Luther that the will is free, and of this view the title of the famous work *De Servo Arbitrio* is exemplary. ' "Free will" constituted apart from grace possesses absolutely no power for righteousness, but necessarily continues in sin.'[6] 'In spiritual and divine things which pertain to the salvation of the soul, man is like the statue of salt into which the wife of the patriarch Lot was turned; nay, rather, he is like a log, a stone, a statue lacking life, which has the use neither of eyes nor of mouth nor of any other sense nor yet of heart.'[7] When elsewhere

---

[1] *Enchir.* 98.   [2] *De corr. et grat.* 14.45.
[3] St Thomas does better than this, for he asks: 'Can there be two agents for one activity?'; and answers: 'that is impossible if the agents are of the same order' (see *ST* I qu. 105, art. 2).
[4] *The Ideas of the Fall and of Original Sin*, London 1927, 429.
[5] Quoted (loc. cit.) from J. A. Quenstedt, *Theologia didactico-polemica*, Wittenberg 1691, vol. II, 134 f.
[6] Quoted in *The Grace of God* from H. Denifle, *Luther und Luthertum*, Mainz 1904–6, 486 n. 2.   [7] *In Genesim*, ch. xix.

Luther says, 'A Christian is a free master over all things and subject to no one; a Christian is a servant at the disposal of all things and subject to every man,' he is clearly talking of a kind of freedom quite different from formal free will.

The consequence of such a position can only be that the work of salvation is wholly to be ascribed to God. Men, sunk as they are in sin, the subjects of 'total depravity', are *pure passivi* until God creates in them by grace a response to this same grace. Predestination is the inevitable conclusion.

This conclusion is indeed associated with Calvin rather than with Luther; and this must be reckoned as one of the oddities of historical theology. Calvin characteristically writes a treatise *De Libero Arbitrio*, and his intention, even in such a work as the *De aeterna Praedestinatione Dei*, was clearly to vindicate the full reality of human action.[1] Yet it was Calvin who outlines and advocates the forbidding doctrine of *predestinatio duplex*. Luther no doubt lacked the systematic interest which would have led him to a similar conclusion, though in many ways it would have been more appropriate to the premises from which he argues.

Here, then, is one interpretation of the relations of grace and freedom. That it possesses a majesty cannot be denied. Nor is it less certain that it sees and expresses a real truth: when salvation is achieved, it can only be rightly represented as a 'gift of God'. But that it is a genuine solution to the problem can hardly be maintained. The chief difficulty is that, dominated as it is by an understanding of grace as some kind of divine force and by a conception of sin which defines man in terms of pure incapacity, the lines have so been drawn that grace is exalted at the cost of man's freedom. But this is to leave the God who exercises grace in his dealings with men out of the reckoning. Then in consequence his nature is misconceived, and a right account of man's place and part cannot be expected.

4. *An alternative statement: Pelagianism and Evangelicalism*

Conceding, then, both the strength and the value of the Augustinian scheme and the schemes that have affinity with it, is it possible to offer an alternative? The answer is in the affirmative: another

[1] See *Concerning the Eternal Predestination of God*, London 1960, Introduction 18 ff., where I have attempted a fuller statement of Calvin's position at this point.

view can be and has been formulated. It is unnecessary to say more than a few words about the position of Pelagius, if only for the reason that it is a direct transcript of what the 'natural man' is all too readily disposed to think—and who of us does not incline to be in this sense 'natural'? The fundamental thesis can be simply stated: 'A man can, if he will, observe God's commandments without sinning.'[1] In support of this thesis, Pelagius comments on two scriptural passages: 'Ye shall be holy, for I am holy' (Lev. 19.2) and: 'Be ye perfect, as your Father in heaven is perfect' (Matt. 5.48), declaring that it would be impious to suggest that God, the Father of all justice, should enjoin what he knows to be impossible.[2] He passes immediately to more contentious grounds when he alleges that Scripture contains many examples of blameless lives.[3] It appears that for practical reasons he repudiated St Augustine's prayer: *Da quod iubes et iube quod vis*,[4] because it seemed to reduce men to mere puppets. On his view, there was in man no ineluctable bias towards evil, and he denied both the necessity and the possibility of a supernatural grace directly assisting man to choose the right. It would be wrong to reject these statements as trivial in themselves and based upon a superficial view of human nature. Pelagius is contending for real and important interests, and for his general understanding of the relation of human freedom and grace he produces two grounds which, in their own place, are weighty. The first is moral: his view offered the only possible alternative to a pessimistic understanding of human nature which could only have demoralizing consequences. The other ground is theological: the autonomy which he accords man does not constitute a denial of God's sovereignty; on the contrary, the freedom of choice which man enjoys is the gift of his Creator and hence he is both obliged and able to use it for the end his Creator prescribes.

It is the grounds just stated that constitute the reason for the persistence of the Pelagian position and for the recurrence of its doctrines in the course of Christian theology. The fact is that evangelical exhortation always tends, when its grounds are not stated with sufficient clarity, to adopt the Pelagian standpoint. Evangelical proclamation involves an appeal to and for faith. In so appealing, it can claim strong scriptural and dominical support, as has already been seen. Our Lord commends faith because it enables

---

[1] St Augustine, *De gest. Pelag.* 16.   [2] *Qualiter* 2.4.
[3] St Augustine, *De nat. et grat.* 42–44.   [4] St Augustine, *De bono persev.* 53.

mighty works to be done, and the apostolic 'Believe and be saved' tends in the same sense. That such exhortation be made is wholly consonant with the general message of Scripture, and it clearly represents an element that is never silent for long.

The more unconsidered forms which this evangelical appeal takes no doubt endorse a simple Pelagianism without conscious resort to the profounder considerations of which Pelagius himself made use. The demand is made for action on the part of those addressed which is independent of and necessarily prior to any particular salvific action on the part of God in their case. But evangelism is not always content to be so unreflective, and the exigencies of the faith by which it lives drive it from the bare Pelagian position. At its best, distinguished perhaps from evangelicalism, evangelism has regularly been aware that, in the last analysis, Pelagianism will not do. It has known that faith does not stand alone and that, so far from being an independent human contribution, it is itself in a real sense the work of God. This complexity is apparent in the greatest evangelical exponents of the Christian faith. St Augustine, for all the emphasis he lays upon the solely efficacious action of God, does not admit that he has rendered human free will nugatory. Hence, when expounding the apparently predestinarian test: 'No man can come to me, except the Father which hath sent me draw him' (John 6.44), he adds the culminating comment:[1] *Nondum traheris? ora ut traheris.* Similarly, against the tendency to elevate the *sola fide* into a position of unique prominence, Luther maintained and reiterated that indeed justification is *sola fide*, but alongside of this he constantly insisted that it had also to be understood as *per Jesum Christum*: if faith belonged to the grounds of justification, it certainly did not comprehend them, nor constituted the sufficient cause of justification.

Further, Luther on the other hand was repeatedly faced with tne charge which the Romanists tried to pin on him, that in the last resort the faith which played so notable a part in the matter of justification was nothing but a human work. Luther thus, it was alleged, fell back into the very error from which he tried to escape; and in this the unreformed Church was in better case, in that it at least referred salvation partly to ecclesiastical ordinances which were not of human contrivance but of God's appointment. But Luther invariably repudiated this reading of his doctrine and repelled the charge, declaring that the faith involved in salvation was

[1] *In Joann. ev.* xxvi.2.

itself the work of God in man and not anything men had to provide out of their own resources. Similarly, in the case of a more recent exponent of evangelism, John Wesley. 'The righteousness of Christ,' he says,[1] 'is doubtless necessary for any soul that enters into glory. But so is personal holiness too, for every child of a man. But it is highly needful to be observed that they are necessary in different respects. The former is necessary to *entitle* us to heaven; the latter to *qualify* us for it. Without the righteousness of Christ, we could have no *claim* to glory; without holiness we could have no *fitness* for it.'

If, then, this represents the true evangelical stream, it is clear that when giving an account of itself the evangelical knows quite well that he cannot cling exclusively to the one side, however important he must make this side appear for practical purposes; and accordingly he is content to fall back upon the simple statement of the two sides. This is not to solve the problem, but to reiterate it. If pressed for greater precision, he might incline to make use of the concept of co-operation, and this would be to adopt something like Synergism. To a consideration of this we now turn.

5. *Synergism*

The Synergistic statement is the one which appears at first glance to offer the readiest refuge, and certainly it is here, wittingly or unwittingly, that many find a standing ground when bewildered by the confusion of competing interests. The characteristic aspects of the Synergistic position may be illustrated from classic exponents. (*a*) As the name implies, some kind of co-operation is involved. When the Formula of Concord came to repudiate the view,[2] it defined it as 'the teaching that, although unregenerate man, in respect of free will, is indeed (antecedently to his regeneration) too infirm to make a beginning of his own conversion, and by his own powers to convert himself to God, and obey the law of God with all his heart; yet, if the Holy Spirit, by the preaching of the Word, shall have made a beginning, and offered his grace in the Word to man, then man, by his own natural and proper powers, can, as it were give some assistance and co-operation (though it be but slight, infirm and languid) towards his conversion, and can apply and prepare

[1] *Sermons*, London 1800, vol. III, 314.
[2] See Schaff, *The Creeds of Christendom*, New York 1878, vol. III, 110 f.

himself unto grace, apprehend it, embrace it, and believe the Gospel.' This states one of the forms in which this human co-operation is expressed: to a beginning made by the divine power, a real contribution can be added out of the resources inherently possessed by man. Alternatively, the contribution may be repre-sented as the withdrawal of impediments to the divine power, or again as the withholding of obstacles to its operation. Thus Melan-chthon, commenting in his work on the Epistle to the Romans upon I Tim. 2.4, 'God willeth that all men should be saved,' declares that this is to be taken in a simple sense: 'the mercy of God is truly the cause of election, but nevertheless there is a certain cause of election in the elected person, in so far as he does not reject God's promise offered to him; for evil arises solely from ourselves.' It is with this possibility in mind that St Augustine draws his distinction between the prevenient grace of God which constitutes the initial impulse which derives from God and without which man cannot even begin to will or to work his salvation, and subsequent or co-operant grace which enables and accompanies good actions after conversion has taken place.

At any rate, as Victorinus Strigel[1] says: 'The regeneration and recreation of man take place not without his own reflection upon the Word and not without some movement of his will.' More systematic-ally, Melanchthon distinguishes[2] three concurrent causes of good action, 'the Word, the Holy Spirit, and the will, not by any means an inert factor, but as fighting against its own weakness'.

(b) This implies that there is something in man which forms the basis of the response which positively promotes a process already initiated, and negatively offers no resistance to the divine power. Thus again there is apparent that certain hypostatization of man over against God, or, to use the language of the second chapter, that substantialization of man, which is so marked and so influential a feature of the whole debate. Man is set up as a substantially indepen-dent agent. The terms used by the Synergists are the same as those used by those who flank them on either side with contrary views: those on the one hand who hold that this independence has simply to be overwhelmed in the matter of salvation, or who hold that it has to be appealed to, evoked and encouraged for the salvific process to make a beginning at all; and on the other hand those prepared to

---

[1] 1524–69, follower of Melanchthon, whose views are to be found in the *Disp. inter Flacium et Strigelium*.   [2] *Loci* (1535), Corpus Reformatorum XXI 376.

H

make terms between the two sides. But when all is said, the terminology remains the same. Man is set up as a substantial agent and as an independent party to be reckoned with; and this understanding of the matter, the Synergist shares with both the Augustinian and the Pelagian. Strigel suggests that man's free will and capacity for goodness are not obliterated but only constricted by the fall and its consequences, like, he says, a magnet which when treated with onion juice cannot exert its magnetic powers though it retains these powers in abeyance. Again, while quite willing to deprecate the size of the contribution that man can make, he wholeheartedly confirms its reality, as when he says: 'It is as if I sat at a banquet, where each guest contributes to the total cost, by the side of a rich man, and he paid a thaler and I a heller.'[1] The will remains intact, is therefore usable, and must be stirred to motion. So too Melanchthon approves of Chrysostom's comment upon John 6.44: 'No man can come to me, except the Father draw him,' when he says: 'Now he that draws draws him who wishes to be drawn.'

(c) Synergists do not necessarily dispense with predestination, but it has to take an appropriate form. The reality which man constitutes forces recognition of itself, and even predestination has to take cognizance of it. The doctrine has therefore to be rewritten in terms of determination *post praevisa merita*. The ground of distinction between the elect and the rejected need not be traced back into the secret counsels of God. It may be discovered much closer at hand: *necesse est in nobis aliquam discriminis causam*. God's judgment of us is 'analytic'.[2]

(d) More practical factors play a part in the development of the views characteristic of Synergism. The movement of Luther's thought is through the elimination of the elements taken over in the inheritance bestowed by the medieval Church, towards a restored realization of the need for emphasis upon God's absolute and sovereign action, and also complementarily upon man's absolute inability. On the other hand, the development discernible in Melanchthon is in the opposite direction. It was possible for him at an early period under the guidance of Luther to make the following statements: 'If you consider the human will in the light of predestination, there is no liberty at all either in outward or in inward

---

[1] See *The Grace of God*, 82.
[2] See Brunner, *The Mediator*, 523 n. 1, criticizing Holl, *Luther* (Gesammelte Aufsätze I), 1927, 124.

deed, but all things come to pass according to the divine ordinance.'[1] And again: 'Not merely does God permit his creatures to act, but he himself is the proper agent in all things that happen; so that as men confess that the conversion of St Paul was God's proper work, so they ought to confess both that morally indifferent actions, such as when men eat, are God's work, and also actions which are bad, like David's adultery: for it is certain that God does all things not permissively, but by his power, so that the treason of Judas was no less his proper work than the conversion of St Paul.'[2] Among the reasons compelling him to resile from a position so rashly occupied were the exigencies of practical and pastoral duties. As has been said, the proclamation of the Gospel is extremely difficult to separate from such hortatory appeals as seem to imply the existence of free will in men and the need for them to make a responsible decision.

There is also apparent in Melanchthon an interest in the phenomenon of conversion, and he makes an early attempt to give some kind of psychological account of it. It is never easy to reconcile this interest with the real independent action of God, as the development of the psychology of religion in modern days has often shown.

(e) Lastly, the whole story has not been told when it is said that Synergism affirms the reality of the human contribution or of the human nature that makes it. The human contribution and the human nature from which it springs are characteristically regarded not only as real but as fundamentally good. *Facienti quod in se est Deus non denegat gratiam*—this affirmation Luther once used in his commentary on the Psalms, but later denounced as 'a most absurd opinion and one which vehemently upholds the Pelagian error'.[3] It is just as characteristic of Synergism. There is that in man of which the work of God must take account and may in a real sense make use. The way is thus opened up for understanding the relation of God and man at this crucial point in terms of supernatural gifts added to natural endowments. It is in these terms that Romanism today still seems to represent the situation. Primitive and unfallen man is held to enjoy this combination. Salvation consists in the recovery of this union of elements. Supernatural grace is superimposed on what is a natural and inalienable possession. This is not only the

---

[1] *Loci* (1521), CR XXI 93 (see *The Grace of God*, 79).
[2] *Comm. ad Rom.* (1525) (see *The Grace of God*, 79 f.).
[3] Denifle, *Luther und Luthertum* I, 553 n. 4 (see *The Grace of God*, 77).

ground of the distinctively human contribution; it also prescribes its character of receptivity. Man initiates nothing, but accepts what is offered from elsewhere, and this is the sphere in which human freedom operates. A certain congruity is thereby achieved with St Paul's 'labourers together with God' (I Cor. 3.9) and the scriptural testimony similar to this. But an implication is to be carefully noted: a residual and unimpaired integrity at least partially preserved within human nature is presupposed. It is this that can be receptive of a supernatural *donum superadditum*, and then further allied and aligned with this supernatural grace given and received.

For those who can accept the view of human nature implied, Synergism supplies the basis on which God's part and man's in the work of salvation can be intelligibly apprehended. But on no other terms will the solution work. This is not the only point at which Roman theology has a ready answer to offer—if only Scripture allowed us to deem it also true.

6. *Faith and the Holy Spirit*

Something must here be said about the work of the Holy Spirit, though it can be no more than brief. As the traditional statement develops, grace is so much and in such a way emphasized as to make it difficult to discern the part that men are called upon to play. The contrary emphasis is evident in Pelagianism, but at the cost of fidelity to the witness of Scripture; while Synergism makes the mistake of attempting to correlate things that do not belong to the same class. But the biblical documents affirm that the faith that is man's response to what God has done in Jesus Christ stands in a relation of dependence to the Holy Spirit. Is it possible that we should look here for enlightenment in the perplexity?

If we are to remain true to this biblical witness, we must certainly say that where faith is the Holy Spirit has been at work. This is clear from passages already cited from St Paul. But the testimony of our Lord is no less clear. No doubt our Lord attributes Peter's pioneering faith to the Father (Matt. 16.18); but this cannot be interpreted as excluding the agency of the Spirit. It is by the Father's revelation that Peter apprehends the messiahship of Jesus. How else could Jesus have rendered glory to God, and how in any other terms made the point that the revelation of God stands in and by its own right? The revelation is the Father's; the *revelatum* is the

Son; and the revelation wins its way in the heart of Peter and of everyone else by the agency of the Spirit.

But the intention of this biblical witness is unmistakable. It is clearly to assert that even faith is the work of God. Certainly the faith in question is yours, or Peter's, or the Corinthians'; but the point made is that wherever faith is it is the work of God in that person. We have seen that the biblical writers seem untroubled by the question how, if faith is God's work, it is also mine or yours or his. They are content to affirm that faith is ours by God's work of the Holy Spirit in us. There is never any suggestion that, because it is the work of God as Holy Spirit to which faith must be ascribed, that therefore it is more distinctly or recognizably ours—rather the reverse: in ascribing it to the Holy Spirit they deliberately withdraw it from among the things for which men can be responsible and over which they have control, in order to place it firmly in God's hands. The Holy Spirit may be said to initiate faith. But even more characteristic of St Paul's thought is that to the Holy Spirit must be ascribed the bestowal of diverse gifts to members of the body of Christ and the consequent production in their lives of the 'fruit of the Spirit'. The Holy Spirit in all this is God's way of working in the human heart enabling it to yield the required Amen in all its fulness; but it is still *God's* way and work. That the Holy Spirit is present to us and with us is certainly true; but that he is some kind of intermediary between God and us is totally false.[1] There is indeed such an intermediary, 'one mediator between God and man, the man Christ Jesus' (I Tim. 2.5). It is Christ that takes men to be in himself, and this is a work objectively accomplished and done for them; and it is within this sphere that the Holy Spirit operates. Christ's work is prior to and wholly excludes man's work. That man *can* respond is due to this that is God's work alone; that he *does* so is due to the Holy Spirit, and this again is God's work.

If we then wish to have what light the Bible has to shed, we must go where the Bible leads. We must trace back as far as we may into God himself *both* his will for men's salvation *and* his will that they should respond. We must look resolutely at predestination.

[1] Calvin can call the Spirit 'the channel by which all that Christ himself is and has is conveyed to us' (*Inst.* 4.17.12). But it is the 'Spirit of Christ' of which he says this, and his words are *quidam veluti canalis*. Much more significant is the fact that it is when stating his eucharistic doctrine that Calvin speaks in this way. Cf. in identical context *Catechism of the Church of Geneva* (see *Calvin: Theological Treatises* [Library of Christian Classics 22], London 1954, 137) and *Consensus Tigurinus* arts. 6, 8, 14–16, 23.

7. *Constructive statement in terms of predestination*

The ordinary man, we may suppose, feels perplexed not only by the problem before us here, but even more by the fact that a problem so radical, so early conceived and so long discussed, has not been provided with a solution with which he can be satisfied. There is indeed no easy solution; yet the lines along which it is possible to see any solution at all are prescribed just when the problem to be solved is present in its apparently most intransigent form. Intellectual break-through often occurs when a problem is stated not in its most amenable but in its most intractable form. This is what happens here when the concept of predestination is applied.

The action of God cannot very well be regarded as merely an improvisation contrived to repair a situation which, without action from outside, is irremediable. It is therefore traced back into the eternal purpose of God, who is then regarded as from all time determining what will be. The *catena salutis*, as St Paul says, not indeed in the *ordo cognoscendi* but in the *ordo essendi*, not in the steps by which we trace the matter back but in the steps in which it issues from God himself, is as follows: 'Whom he did foreknow, he also did predestinate, . . . whom he did predestinate, them he also called: and whom he called, them he also justified: and whom he justified, them he also glorified' (Rom. 8.29 f.). Then indeed it appears that the absolute sovereignty of God is fully safeguarded. But, in the course of the debate, it is safeguarded in terms that make it wellnigh impossible to retain for men's action any independent reality, and human freedom seems to be hopelessly compromised and in the end surrendered.

Here undoubtedly the tendency to regard divine grace in terms of power operated mischievously. As already said, St Augustine is content to regard the power of God over men's wills as simply greater than the power men have themselves over them. According to N. P. Williams[1] and Loofs, the actual word irresistible does not occur in what St Augustine writes; but when he says: '*Subventum est igitur infirmitati voluntatis humanae, ut divina gratia indeclinabiliter et insuperabiliter ageretur,*'[2] the idea of irresistibility is unmistakably present. But is this idea of grace as irresistible power in any sense compatible, we will not say with men's freedom, but with the reality of men's independent action? When St Augustine is faced

---

[1] Op. cit. 26.   [2] *De corr. et grat.* 12.38.

with this question, he is unwilling to give a negative answer. But the characteristic retort he makes, and it is one which especially Calvin after him repeatedly uses, is an appeal to the Pauline 'O homo, tu quis es?' of Rom. 9.20. With the advent of the idea of predestination, the general problem of the relation between grace and freedom, between God and man, is indeed transposed into a different and sublimer key. But the only use made of this transposition is to indicate that in this sublimer sphere there is an answer, but it is impious to inquire what it is.

That any other use can be made of this transposition of the problem to a sublimer key will not be realized so long as predetermination is regarded as nothing else than a greater degree of determination. 'Anything that is completely determined from outside itself,' says N. H. G. Robinson,[1] 'is deprived of all spontaneity, and must be conceived as wholly passive and entirely impressionable'—with this statement in itself there can be no quarrel. But it has nothing whatever to do with predestination. The fact is that the difference between determination and predestination is not one of degree but of kind; and it has been the fateful identification of grace with some kind of impersonal force that has so often impeded the realization of this truth. We have to take quite seriously the fact that the divine determination is always conceived in Scripture as strictly predetermination, even where, as for instance in Luke 22.22 and Acts 17.26, it is not verbally designated as such; and that therefore it is not merely a more than usually adamant determination. To employ the *analogia entis* at this point instead of the *analogia fidei* can only lead to error. I. T. Ramsey[2] sets the problem in at least a correct light when, considering for example the omnipotence of God, he regards the 'all' as a 'qualifier', transposing what follows into a different key. We may perhaps venture to give an example coming from quite another field but illustrating the point at issue. B. J. F. Lonergan writes[3] as follows: 'Gödel's theorem is to the effect that any set of mathematical definitions and postulates gives rise to further questions that cannot be answered on the basis of the definitions and postulates. . . . The really significant context is the upper context; all lower contexts . . . are provisional; and they attain a definite significance only in the measure that they give access to the upper context.' *Mutatis mutandis*, when we are dealing with scriptural

---

[1] *Christ and Conscience*, London 1956, 193.
[2] *Freedom and Immortality*, London 1960, 57 f.   [3] *Insight*, London 1958, xxv.

predestination, we have to let the 'upper context' speak for itself, even if in explaining itself it must make use of different terms from those which suffice upon the 'lower context'.

Predestination, then, so far from doing more than anything else to obliterate freedom, provides the context in which alone man's free and independent action is possible or conceivable. God neither shares independence with his creation, nor limits his freedom in order to create a sphere for its freedom.[1] We must really stop thinking that there is a field of operation to be divided, so that the more we assign to God the less there is for us to do, and the more we arrogate to ourselves the smaller the part God has to play. In fact philosophical considerations alone might correct us here. For we are dealing with two incommensurable terms, finite man and infinite God. Between two such incommensurables, there is and can be no point-for-point correspondence, for the principle of correspondence applies only to finite magnitudes. To use the famous metaphor, we may not compare God and man to two men launching a boat, where if one does less work the other has to do more. God is not like a schoolmaster who withdraws in order to test his pupils' ability and knowledge; nor is he like a bureaucrat who grudges every sign of individual and independent action because it encroaches upon his own sphere of office. God is the true aristocrat,[2] so fearless concerning his own authority and majesty that he takes pleasure in the real possibility of individual actions and events, and in predestination he supplies the conditions in which they can occur.

8. *Predestination in Christ*

We must first understand that it is God who operates predestination. If we hold this firmly, we shall certainly relinquish the errant development which characterizes so much of the traditional discussion of predestination, the error that grace can be hypostatized and credited with a separate and independent existence apart from God. 'God's presence and his very self/And essence all-divine' is not, as Newman's well-known hymn[3] would have us believe, 'a higher gift than grace'. The two are primarily synonymous. It may be that we cannot turn back the clock and insist that the Pauline under-

[1] Hence Calvin's steady denial that God's will may be divided into an executive will and a permissive will.
[2] See Karl Barth, *Kirchliche Dogmatik* III/3 156 (Eng. trs. 138).
[3] 'Praise to the Holiest in the height . . .'

standing of grace as simply divine favour is its sole legitimate meaning. But we must regard other meanings as secondary and derivative,
and resist the tendency to credit grace with an independence of God
which it does not possess.

Further, as at other points, so here too we have to understand
that the God who operates predestination is the God and Father of
our Lord Jesus Christ. This can mean nothing else than that it is
the God of grace who is also the God of predestination. We must
say that we know that God is gracious through Jesus; but we must
also add that in him the grace of God comes to meet us.

It follows that, as grace is not to be separated from God, so predestination must not be separated from Jesus Christ. It is at this
point that a certain weakness appears in some of the classic exposi-
tions of predestination. In St Augustine this is manifest in the
appeal to the '*O homo, quis tu es?*' with which he too peremptorily
and precipitately stifles inquiry. If one is then left with the impression
that there are depths in God which are simply inscrutable, this is
the consequence of irresolution in carrying to its proper limits the
revelation of God which we have in Jesus Christ. In Calvin this
irresolution is also apparent. It is true that he follows St Paul in
affirming that God 'hath chosen us in [Jesus Christ] before the
foundation of the world' (Eph. 1.4). It is true that he regards Christ
as 'the bright mirror of the eternal and hidden election of God', as
the 'earnest and pledge', and as the 'seal' of our determination, and
as the *ratio cognoscendi* of our election by God.[1] But he also makes a
distinction between Christ as the 'manner in which God discharges
his work of grace' and the 'superior cause' of his taking the elect
by the hand;[2] and he can even say:[3] '*gratiam istam Dei praecedit
electio.*'[4] If this is so, then the primary ground of our predestination
is to be found in the *divinae sapientiae adyta* where it is lodged in an
arcanum consilium; and, though Christ is recognized as the *instru-
mentum* of our election, Calvin manifests a hesitancy in expressly
declaring him to be also its *fundamentum*.[5] This weakness can only
be corrected by a more thorough application of Eph. 1.4 to the

---

[1] These metaphors occur in *Concerning the Eternal Predestination of God*, §VIII.
6 *et al.*   [2] Op. cit. §VIII.4.   [3] *Inst.* 3.22.1.

[4] Perhaps too much emphasis should not be laid on this phrase, since the grace
referred to seems to be sanctifying grace which Calvin may in some unusual way be
distinguishing as a subsequent operation of grace in general. The text is: *Si gratiam
istam Dei, ut idonei ad gloriam futurae vitae obtinendam reddamur, praecedit electio:
quid iam reperiet in nobis Deus ipse, quo ad eligendos moveatur?*

[5] See *Concerning the Eternal Predestination of God*, Introduction 4.3.

doctrine of predestination. If what St Paul says there is true, then Christ must unhesitatingly be declared to be privy to the counsel of the Father and to be along with him the author of predestination.

But this is not all; for Jesus Christ is not only the author but also the subject of predestination. Of this the first recorded Christian sermon is evidence. In Acts 2.23, St Peter speaks of 'him being delivered by the determinate counsel and foreknowledge of God'. Nor does this evidence stand alone: there are dominical words that witness in the same sense. 'Truly the Son of man goeth, as it was determined' (Luke 22.22); 'Ought not Christ to have suffered these things, and to enter into his glory?' (Luke 24.26 f.); 'From that time forth began Jesus to shew unto his disciples, how that he must go unto Jerusalem, and suffer many things of the elders and chief priests and scribes, and be killed, and be raised again the third day' (Matt. 16.21). Here too belong the solemn references to his 'hour', negatively that it is not yet come (John 7.30; 8.20), and positively that it was upon him (Matt. 26.45; 14.35; Luke 22.14, 53; John 12.23; 17.1; 13.1, and especially 12.27). Jesus Christ is thus the prototype of predestination. It is with this intention that Calvin, as already said, recognizes in him 'the bright mirror of the eternal and hidden counsel of God',[1] and 'the most excellent luminary of grace and predestination'.[2] And Barth has to be cited as responsible in recent times for reminding Christian theology of this truth— '*Jesus Christus ist der Erwählende und der Erwählte.*'[3]

And now still another thing has to be added. We have been facing the apparently intransigent problem of relating God's action with men's, or alternatively of so relating the sovereignty of God as not to obliterate the real if also relative independence of men. In the case of one single Person, the problem is not only theoretically solved but is in actual practice dissolved. This single Person is of course Jesus Christ. He who is the prototype of predestination is at the same time he who renders a perfect independent response: on the one hand 'it is written of him', but on the other, as he himself states, 'the Son of man goeth' (Matt. 26.24). He who is the grace of God incarnate perfectly obeys him who sent him. On the testimony of the Fourth Gospel, the pattern according to which our Lord lives His life is: 'I must work the works of him that sent me' (John 9.4);

---

[1] Op. cit. §VIII.6.   [2] Op. cit. §IV.

[3] *Kirchliche Dogmatik* II/2—one long subsection under §33 carries this title ('Jesus Christ, Electing and Elected') and is devoted to exposition of the theme.

and the rubric under which he ends it is: 'I have finished the work which thou gavest me to do' (John 17.4). In him there is perfect congruity between the action of God and the action of man.

To say all difficulty thereby disappears would be not only to say too much but to conceive the matter wrongly. In Jesus Christ the problem is resolved practically, and action divine and human have moved into coincidence with one another. In a sense this only amounts to a shifting of the point of impact of the element of paradox. It now appears not where action divine and human are concerned, but in the God-man himself; and the residual mystery concerns not his nature itself, but more strictly the way in which that nature was brought about. This is indeed the final and ultimate paradox, that God becomes incarnate. And yet that it has been shifted there is of the greatest importance, and offers considerable help to our understanding.

For now the fact appears that where this Man is we also are. This has been the main burden of what has here been said. Let us express the matter once more. Rom 4.24 f. and II Cor. 5.18 have already been cited as scriptural statement of the problem with which we are here concerned. But in their earlier citation the exposition was unduly simplified. It was represented as though there were only two factors in the case, God and man. Thus God imputes righteousness to us—if we believe on him that raised up Jesus; God has reconciled—therefore be you reconciled. But there is in fact in both cases a third factor explicitly named—the factor (if we may so speak) that is Jesus Christ himself. When this is taken into account, we must in justice amplify the statement of what Scripture is saying: God imputes righteousness to us—if we believe on him that raised Jesus up—who was delivered for our offences and was raised again for our justification; and: God has reconciled—therefore be you reconciled—(and again the third factor) for Jesus Christ was made to be sin for us that we might be the righteousness of God in him. The apostle is clearly at pains to point out that it is not God and we alone that are concerned, but rather God and we and Jesus Christ. He thus invites us to take with the seriousness that has been attempted here the effectualness of the role that Jesus Christ plays.

But the exact character of the role is still more carefully defined, as we have already had reason to observe. We do not rightly conceive that role when we think of Jesus as procuring for men certain salvific benefits, and, himself standing apart from them, as proffering these benefits to them. He is not himself distinct from the offered benefits; and the Gospel consists in an invitation not so much to accept certain benefits procured on their behalf, as to be in him and thereby to enjoy with, by and in him the benefits he offers. We are invited not to accept proffered gifts, but rather to be in him; for the Father gives us all things richly to enjoy in him (I Tim. 6.17). To the fact that Christ applies what he procures to us, the 'in Christ' adds that he applies also what he is to us.

When we ask what in the work of salvation we must attribute to God and what to man, we ask a question that is not fully Christian.[1] In Jesus Christ, the paradox of grace and freedom, of God's action and man's, is overcome and an example provided of their perfect coincidence. But of course Jesus Christ is not merely an example. The fact that in him the paradox is overcome has not merely theoretical value but also soteriological value. In other words, what Jesus Christ is at this point, he is for us. When the Bible wants to express this as a fact, it presents Jesus Christ to us, incarnate, crucified, risen and regnant. In this presence, what we have to do and the faith we have to offer is not a problem; and this is so because we are not merely in his presence but in him.

When, however, the Bible wishes to conduct us a little further into an understanding of the mystery, as sometimes it does, then it declares: 'God hath chosen us in Christ Jesus before the foundation of the world . . . having predestinated us unto the adoption of

---

[1] The problem must be rightly apprehended before we can begin to talk about it as 'wearisome'. Karl Barth (*Kirchliche Dogmatik* III/3 213 f. [Eng. trs. 188 f.]) says: 'What is the relationship between the freedom of God and that of the creature? With all its wearisomeness the question will flare up again and again as long as hazy notions prevail concerning who or what we mean by God, as long as we answer the question in another way than the Christian. But where God is at work in the supremacy of his free grace, where the King of Israel is active with his Word and act to and by his people as opposed to the world at large, there we really see the two in a single relationship . . . which is inwardly calm and positive . . . [The history of salvation] does not offer any solution at all to the technical problem raised. If we read the Bible with a desire to find any such solution, we shall find that it has nothing to say. But it offers us something far greater and far better, the fact of a relationship between the Creator and his creatures, between his freedom and their freedom, which is still clear and positive in spite of the existence of this problem. If we look at this factual relationship, and therefore at the rule of God in Israel, we see that it is actually true that in the world-governance of God everything has to be and is absolutely under God, and yet everything attains in freedom to its own validity and honour.' Here Barth is surely right. Faith is not a problem on the practical level. We do not give up faith because we cannot understand how it is related to God's action. If there is an intellectual problem, and if the intellectual problem is an obstacle to anyone's responding in faith, then the example of Jesus Christ is a solvent: in him God's action and man's coincide.

children by Jesus Christ, to himself' (Eph. 1.4 f.). Thus the grace of God sets forth Jesus Christ for us, and he will see us only in him. What Jesus Christ exemplifies in history before our eyes, is laid up in him for us in all eternity. We have therefore to predicate of the status accorded to us in Christ Jesus an impregnable security. On God's side, it is not merely a more or less effective improvisation, but is grounded with all the lasting stability that predestination imparts. On our side, it is quite separated, in its basis though not of course in its exercise, from subjective piety and the vagaries of personal faith.[1] It will be necessary to look at some of the implications involved by this very security in the chapter that follows.

[1] So W. Schmauch, Ἐν Χριστῷ, 66: 'In all passages without exception, the ἐν Χριστῷ Ἰησοῦ denotes a divine event quite independent of the life of faith and laid down in eternal completeness which, as Phil. 3.3, permits only a relation to history that adds nothing to its significance but is rather determined by it, the glory which is the echo of the divine deed.'

6

The Consummation of the Life

1. *The entire Christian life is in Christ*

THE life in Christ is a condition or status into which men are primarily assumed in virtue of what Jesus Christ has done for them. The validity or effectiveness of what he does is not dependent upon what they themselves do, as though it needed supplement or completion from elsewhere. Of course there is need of faith. But faith is not to be regarded as a condition to be fulfilled before what he has done applies to us. On the contrary, faith only becomes possible because of what has already been done for us by him.[1] To put it in other terms, we do not have to go half-way to meet one who offers us the gift of this life. We have rather been already by him brought all the way, and being in him the gifts he has are ours. As St Paul precisely says, we have 'grace bestowed on us in the Beloved' (Eph. 1.6 Moffatt). There remains only for us to be what we are. Our whole life is characterized by its being in Christ.

The Pauline Epistles provide abundant evidence of the competence of Christ to sustain the role thus assigned to him. We have already seen that the living are held together in oneness by their being in Christ. But there are also others who are no longer with us: there are 'the dead in Christ' (I Thess. 4.16). What chiefly characterized them in their life here is still their salient feature when life is at an end. They are in Christ now, and if their rising is delayed, it will when the time comes be also in Christ. This comes to more precise expression in I Cor. 15.18, 20, where it is asserted first that there are those 'which are fallen asleep in Christ'; and then that, as they fell asleep, so they are to wake: 'in Christ shall all be made

---

[1] Fritz Neugebauer (*In Christus*) rightly points out, in opposition to Bultmann with his emphasis on faith as decision, that St Paul never makes faith the subject of an imperative: with him it is never '*pisteuete*', but rather 'stand fast in the faith' (I Cor. 16.13) (165). 'What is determined by "in Christ" is expressed in faith' (171); both 'in Christ' and faith represent indicatives (174).

alive.' The same principle is at work both here and hereafter: that which was theirs will also be theirs, and in Christ their future is assured. The whole path of the Christian is plotted out for him already in Christ. For God 'hath chosen us in him before the foundation of the world, that we should be holy and without blame before him in love' (Eph. 1.4); 'for we are his workmanship, created in Christ Jesus unto good works, which God hath before ordained that we should walk in them' (Eph. 2.10). Further, Eph. 1.10: 'that in the dispensation of the fulness of times he might gather together in one all things in Christ, both which are in heaven and which are on earth; even in him: in whom we have obtained an inheritance.' The thought is that not only is the beginning of our course bound up with its being in Christ, not only is its continuance in Christ, but its end too is comprehended by this phrase; and again not only our end, but the end of 'all things'. It is notable that the very phrase 'in Christ', in and by which St Paul commends Christ in all his nearness and intimacy to the Christians to whom he writes, is the very phrase used to designate also the unexampled greatness, majesty and exaltation of his dominion over all things. The poorest and least successful Christian is in Christ; and at the consummation it will be apparent that all things are gathered up in him.

The scope of the life of the man in Christ is then based upon a ground with these dimensions. But St Paul adds greater precision to this conception. To think of Christ as having to do with us at the beginning of the Christian career, and all through it, and also at its end is still not enough. The 'in Christ' is more stringently applied to the Christian career. Christ does not merely make a series of incidental and transient contacts with the Christian; in a real sense the man in Christ reduplicates the career of Christ himself. There is even a point-to-point correspondence. For the career of the Christian may be divided into three stages which have as correlates three salient moments in the career of Christ. The key passage is Rom. 6.3 ff.: 'Know ye not, that so many of us as were baptized into Jesus Christ were baptized into his death? Therefore we are buried with him in baptism into death: that like as Christ was raised up from the dead by the glory of the Father, even so we also should walk in newness of life. For if we have been planted together in the likeness of his death, we shall be also in the likeness of his resurrection: knowing this, that our old man is crucified with him, that the body of sin might be destroyed, that henceforth we should not serve sin. Now if we be dead with Christ, we believe that we shall also live with him: knowing that Christ being raised from the dead dieth no more; death hath no more dominion over him. For in that he died, he died unto sin once: but in that he liveth, he liveth unto God. Likewise reckon ye also yourselves to be dead indeed unto sin, but alive unto God through Jesus Christ our Lord.' Analysis of this passage reveals what the three stages are. (a) In Christ the Christian dies—the affirmations of vv. 6, 8 and 11 are intensified by the reference to burial, as though at this point too there is a parallelism; and they are complemented by 'for ye are dead, and your life is hid with Christ in God' (Col. 3.3). But (b), at times almost in the same breath, St Paul is already bringing forward the second stage: the Christian is also alive and is this also in Christ Jesus. He parallels Christ in his rising from the dead, as at vv. 4 and 11; and these passages are complemented by the categorical statement of II Cor. 5.17: 'therefore if any man be in Christ he is a new creature: old things are passed away; behold, all things are become new.' To this there succeeds (c) a third stage: the Christian has not only a newness of life in the present but an assured future, and as the one has its correlate in the resurrection of Christ so the other is related to his exaltation. The fact of this assured future is stated at v. 8, where the second stage is elided, as St Paul hurries on to the future state. Its correlation with the exaltation of Christ appears elsewhere: 'for ye are dead, and your life is hid with Christ in God. When Christ, who is our life, shall appear, then shall ye also appear with him in glory' (Col. 3.3 f.); 'for if by one man's offence death reigned by one; much more they which receive abundance of grace and of the gift of righteousness shall reign in life by one, Jesus Christ' (Rom. 5.17).[1]

The close identification of the man who is in Christ with Christ's career is clearly not the end product of a deliberate effort of imitation. The rubric of baptism under which it is represented would alone suffice to dismiss any such idea. St Paul has selected his

---

[1] Rom. 6.3 ff. is not the only passage witnessing to this three-point correlation of the Christian's career with Christ, though in it the correlation is worked out most clearly in terms of the 'in Christ'. Closely corresponding parallels are found at II Cor. 5.14–17 and Col. 3.3 f., each making a contribution of its own. In the first, v. 16, the dispensability of relation with Christ 'after the flesh' is affirmed, and this validates relation with the resurrected and exalted Christ and makes possible participation in both his resurrection and his exaltation. In the second, the Christian's career is expressed with great clarity and brevity: the Christian is dead, has life, and shall appear in glory. The strand of baptism, woven into Rom. 6.3 ff., is absent from the two parallel passages cited, but it reappears at Col. 2.12.

metaphor with care and propriety. For baptism stands at the initiation of the life of the Church member, is normally done without the voluntary consent of the baptizand, and really effects something incommensurable with the human actions involved. In any case, the reduplication is conceived as reiterating precisely these moments in the career of Christ which remain outside the reach of human imitation. The disciples of Jesus followed him with varying degrees of fidelity during his earthly life. This following is abruptly broken off at the crucifixion. If there is a resumption, it is a new start made after rupture. With the new beginning then made, the following takes on an entirely different character. It is no longer the external copying which the imitator has to contrive; it has rather been contrived for us, and into that contrivance we have been admitted. A disciple's conscious imitation of Jesus is stopped short at the cross, in order that on the far side it may be resumed as a humble working out of the fundamental likeness to the career of Christ which has been imparted to his career.

The general conception is then that the life in Christ has its past grounded in the death of Christ, its present in the resurrection of Christ, and its consummation in the exaltation of Christ. It would be unwarrantable to try to dragoon all that St Paul has to say about the life in Christ so as to conform rigidly to this pattern. There are passages where the lines of distinction in the scheme are blurred. If, in the crucial passage in Romans quoted above, the future tense is ordinarily to be taken as referring to the third and culminating stage, and if this in other passages is confirmed, for example by the further characterization of 'reigning' (Rom. 5.17), it is puzzling that at v. 5 the past likeness to Christ's death is paralleled by a future likeness to his resurrection, where we should expect rather his glory or exaltation as correlate. This can only mean that St Paul is not in the first place concerned with systematic neatness. There is in fact a sufficient regularity in his terminology to warrant taking quite seriously the pattern suggested, and eliciting from it what is possible. If the consummation of the life in Christ is really a third stage and linked to Christ's glory and exaltation, light will be thrown upon it by the other two stages it succeeds, where the past of the life in Christ is related to Christ's death, and the present life in Christ is related to Christ's resurrection. To a brief consideration of the three stages in this order we now turn.

2. *Reduplication of the death of Christ*

The man in Christ reduplicates[1] the death of Christ. The word reduplication could easily be misunderstood. There can of course be no thought of repetition or doubling. The term replica would in some ways be more fitting; but this probably errs just as seriously on the side of vagueness. What is involved is neither a repetition nor a wan imitative shadow or facsimile. St Paul is much more direct and realistic in his language. His thought is that the man in Christ enters into Christ's death;[2] and it is best to leave the matter stated thus.

By entering into the death of Christ, the man in Christ has his past dealt with. Here two questions arise: how does Christ deal with this past? and how is the man in Christ so joined in this death that it becomes the prelude to his new life? Of the first question, little need here be said. What the death of Christ has done to deal with a man's past has exercised a continual fascination for theological thought, and there have been many attempts, each in its own way illuminating, to categorize the ways in which it has historically been represented. It is familiar ground that these ways can be represented according to the metaphor employed, whether it be the camp or the temple or the law-court:[3] according to the role Christ is understood to have played, as substitute, representative or example;[4] according to the status from which men are delivered, that is as accused by justification, as enemy by reconciliation, as debtor by forgiveness, as slave by redemption, as alien by adoption;[5] or more simply as the Eastern and the Western, the latter distinguished by the emergence of the forensic idea of sin as transgression of law.[6] But for the purpose here, the controlling thought is that what was done in the death is prelude to a further stage, and that the risen life which constitutes this second stage is reached through the death that is died. This representation is expressed by the view which G. Aulén has designated the classic view. As D. M. Baillie

---

[1] If Jesus Christ according to Irenaeus recapitulates the whole career of humanity (*Haer*. III.18.1 *et al.*), we may dare to say that the man in Christ in some sense recapitulates the whole career of our Lord himself.

[2] This is not a mere metaphor, any more than baptism, the idea interwoven into the argument here, is a mere ineffective symbol.

[3] See A. B. Macaulay, *The Death of Jesus*, London 1938, 169 ff.

[4] See J. K. Mozley, *The Doctrine of the Atonement*, London 1915, 173 f.

[5] See A. Deissmann, *Paul*, 167 ff.

[6] See A. G. Hebert's Introduction to G. Aulén, *Christus Victor*, Eng. trs., London 1931, v.

states it,[1] 'the atonement is essentially, from start to finish, the costly but victorious conflict of God himself, in Christ, with the forces of evil.'

We may therefore take the view represented by *Christus Victor* to be normative as we proceed to face the second question and ask: how does what Christ does in his death (and resurrection) involve us? We are concerned no longer with anything that we may be supposed or required to do. The question is being asked at a deeper level. What is done is done objectively and by Christ for us, without our being asked, and without our being obliged to do anything at all. At this level, it is a divine work with which we are concerned. Thus the question is how we are by Christ and in Christ made to participate in what is done. The biblical answer is furnished by St Paul: 'as in Adam . . . so in Christ' (I Cor. 15.22).[2] St Paul thus falls back upon the solidarity of the human race. This solidarity is taken with the utmost seriousness. It is to be understood not only as the basis of our participation in what Adam does (the fall) and in what Christ does (his death), but as the basis also of our participation in the consequences that flow from each, the death which Adam incurred and the victorious life which Christ gains.

For an age marked as is the present by the influence of individualism, it is not so easy to conceive how we may properly be said to be involved in what Adam did and incurred. Even St Augustine was troubled by the question. Though he inclined to the creationist view of the origin of the individual soul, he admitted that the traducianist view supplies a readier explanation of how Adam's successors are involved in his act and its consequences. In modern days, it may be that the disastrous practical consequences that have followed from an economic and political employment of the principle of *laissez faire* are showing us the inadequacy of an individualism too uncritically accepted. However this may be, our solidarity with Christ does not present an equal difficulty. If God has really 'chosen us in him', then we must accept that God deals with us in virtue of that relation with him into which he has assumed us.

Yet care has to be taken here too. The very objectivity of Christ's

---

[1] *God was in Christ*, 200.

[2] It is true that in this verse St Paul passes immediately from our participation in Adam's death to our participation in Christ's life. But it is not illegitimate to fill out this summary outline by what he says in Rom. 6.4. It then appears that we participate not only in Adam's fatal death but also in Christ's salvific death, and are thus brought to participation in his life.

work which he does for us and without us may give occasion for doubt whether our participation in his victorious death has been adequately secured. It is all too easy to fall back upon the conception that, Christ winning his victory, he simply invites us to enjoy its fruits. What then Christ has done is to overcome a racial disability. As Adam involves the race, so Christ exculpates the race. Then the real beneficiary of Christ's work is the race as such, just as the victory is won over the cosmic sin and death in which the race has been involved. This would imply that Christ has by his death won salvation for us in principle. But we should still have to wrestle with the question how this principle applies to real men. Here we ought to listen to what D. M. Baillie has to say:[1] 'In the theological argument on this subject we are apt to forget that we are dealing with a realm of personal relationships and nothing else.' If this is so, we must abandon the attempt to represent what Christ has done as though it was in principle alone that sin and death had been conquered. We must affirm that not only the principle but also the application of the principle is safely in his hands. A. G. Hebert declares[2] that one of the notable features of Aulén's *Christus Victor* is his reassertion that 'it is God himself who in Christ has delivered mankind from the power of evil'. There is no victory in principle which has subsequently to be applied to us. By his death, we are taken in Christ to an awareness of what sin really is at the very moment when it is effectively dealt with. For there Christ was made sin in order that he might conquer sin. But this conquest is not to be represented only as though some alien power was being defeated, however valuable this representation may for certain purposes be. For 'God was in Christ, reconciling the world unto himself, not imputing their trespasses unto them' (II Cor. 5.19). The death which Christ died has become our death to all that is past. Forgiveness turns the blotted page and a clean sheet is offered. We pass through the death he died to the life to which he is raised.

3. *Reduplication of the rising of Christ*

The man in Christ reduplicates the rising of Christ. Certain passages in which this is made clear have already been cited. One stage of the Christian's career has been made incontestably secure: by Christ's death and his participation in this death, he has been

---

[1] *God was in Christ*, 198.　　　　　　[2] *Christus Victor*, v.

vindicated against his past. The future stage has still to be manifested. Between these two stages, there is intercalated the Christian's
present. This is the stage in which the Christian, according to
St Paul, is alive with a life that reduplicates Christ's rising from the
dead. As the stage following that at which entry to the Christian
life has been given, and prior to that of which he has as yet only
expectation, this stage has its own special features. If there are
problems too, they are not precipitated by St Paul's schematism.
On the contrary, the schematism is an attempt to do justice to the
special problems which Christians here and now, in their every-day
life, have to face. 'Being confident of this very thing, that he which
hath begun a good work in you will perform it until the day of
Jesus Christ' (Phil. 1.6)—St Paul, as he looks forward to the future,
characterizes the present: it is the age in which progress and advance
is to be made in the Christian life. As he says, 'we also should walk
in newness of life' (Rom. 6.4). The factual identity of Christians in
the death of Christ is succeeded by their identity with the risen
life of Christ which is a matter not of fact alone but of obligation:
the actual is for the time being displaced by (if we may use the
word) the ideal, the already contrived by that which is to be accomplished. Those who *are* 'risen with Christ' have in this state to
'*seek* those things that are above' (Col. 3.1).

The correlate in the career of Jesus Christ is apparent. Between
him who died on the cross and him who rose again 'by the glory
of the Father' (Rom. 6.4) or 'by [God's] own power' (I Cor. 6.14),
there is a difference designated by the *noli tangere* (John 20.17).
In the earlier state, men could work their will upon him (Acts 2.23);
in the later, he has gone beyond their sphere of influence. He who
was made 'to be sin for us, who knew no sin' (II Cor. 5.21), who
again 'was in all points tempted like as we are' (Heb. 4.15) and so
died, is now withdrawing from that identity with us as we are, in
order to go before us. His substantial identity with us is replaced
by an ideal identity. What he did for us has now at last to be
implemented. No one, however much he emphasized the objectivity
and completeness of what Christ has done for us, ever suggested
that there is nothing left for us to do at any point. The sphere of
scriptural exhortation, of Pauline pleading, of the strictly Christian
ethical imperative, is at this point reached. Not, if we may venture
to say it again, that anything requires to be added to what Christ
has done for us once for all. But what he has done has now, not

indeed to be supplemented, but only implemented. There is all the difference in the world between making effective what Christ did and putting into effect what Christ did. Christ has already done the first once for all; the second is now left to those who benefit by what has thus been done.

Not that they are left to do this on their own. We have had little to say so far about the Holy Spirit. This has not been due to oversight but to deliberation. The phrase 'in Christ' has been our guide throughout, and the design has been to represent what Christ has done in the full objectivity and completeness which it rightly possesses. More often than not, the pattern of the Christian faith is represented as though there was a work effected by Christ for me but apart from me, which therefore has by some means to be applied to me; and this work of application is assigned to the Holy Spirit. This representation disregards the Pauline conception of 'in Christ', both in its eternal mode in which our determination in Christ is a divine appointment already made, and also in its temporal mode in which the work of Christ must be seen as something already directly implicating us. Christ's work is our translation to a standing in him, and between the work and its effecting there is no separation which has to be made good by the Holy Spirit. If we allow ourselves to be guided by the conception 'in Christ', it is untenable to regard the work of Christ as effecting something whose application to us is then allotted to another agent, namely the Holy Spirit. The words of our Lord are specific enough: it is the Son of man who 'came to give his life a ransom for many' (Matt. 20.28). It is indeed not the Father who does this work, but neither is it the Holy Spirit.

But the Holy Spirit does have a function here. It is the work of sanctification, of producing fruit in the case of those who have been transplanted by the work of Christ to be in him, of enabling them to work out the status which has been made theirs. The common phrase runs: Handsome is that handsome does; but in the Christian context, the order is reversed; it is: Handsome does that handsome is. This last we have been made; but the aid of the Holy Spirit is with us enabling us to be what we are. The 'fruit' of which St Paul speaks is that 'of the Spirit', summarily described in Eph. 5.9, and in greater detail in Gal. 5.22. The qualities mentioned in the latter passage are the product of the man who, being effectively transferred to a status in Christ, is fructified by the Holy Spirit working in him.

Nor should it be supposed that it is upon an individualistic basis that this is done. No doubt sanctification must take place in the individual life, as a fine harvest can only come from single stalks each yielding fruit. But it has to be remembered that the Spirit is not only the sanctifier but also the bestower of gifts. The gifts are indeed diverse, but they are bestowed upon those that are members of the body of Christ, largely for exercise within that body (I Cor. 12.12; Eph. 4.12). St Paul can even speak of 'the unity of the Spirit' (Eph. 4.3), though oneness is more commonly ascribed to Christ himself (Gal. 3.28). Those in Christ have a life from him which manifests itself in the employment of those special and individual competences which it is the work of the Spirit both to impart and to enable.

It is of importance too that St Paul includes among the 'fruit of the Spirit' (Gal. 5.22) faith itself. This endorses what was said earlier: faith is subsequent to our being in Christ, and has nothing to do with prior conditions which must first be supplied. Once again men are not required to go half-way to meet their Saviour with faith in their hands. He has come all the way to them and admits them to himself, and from this springs 'all joy and peace in believing' (Rom. 15.13).

4. Reduplication of the exaltation of Christ

The man in Christ reduplicates the exaltation of Christ. The passage to this third section has already been made. If the second stage is subject to the categories of advance and improvement, the third stage, if we trust the faithfulness of God, must lead to consummation. On the witness of St Paul, we have good grounds for such a trust, for he himself speaks of being 'confident of this very thing, that he which hath begun a good work in you will perform it until the day of Jesus Christ' (Eph. 1.6). There is, then, really no question about the completion of the work begun for us and so in us; the only question to be raised is how we ought to conceive the completion.

It is tempting to think of the terms 'in Christ' and 'with Christ' as referring respectively to the two stages and as characteristic and so illuminative of them and of the difference between them. But the terminology of St Paul does not allow of such strict differentiation. The passage Rom. 6.3 ff. quoted above as cardinal in the determination of the second stage forbids us to make the distinction along these lines in any simple fashion. The conception 'with Christ' obtrudes too prominently into both the first stage and the second. We are 'buried with him' in baptism, 'crucified with him', 'dead with Christ'; and again we are 'buried with him' in baptism (Col. 2.12) and 'crucified with him' (Gal. 2.20). Moreover the second stage is sometimes designated in the same terms: we are to expect that we 'shall also live with him' (Rom. 6.8), 'risen with him through the faith of the operation of God who raised him from the dead' (Col. 2.12), and 'risen with Christ' (Col. 3.1). Both first and second stages in the Christian's career are thus designated in terms not only of 'in Christ' but also of 'with Christ'. There is thus multiplicity in the way in which St Paul describes them: 'in Christ' is used and could adequately cover these cases, but the fact is that St Paul also uses 'with Christ' to expound what he has to say about them.

But there is only one phrase which he uses to designate the third stage of the Christian's career. In this relation, the 'in Christ' quite drops out and is replaced by the 'with Christ', and this becomes the regular way in which St Paul refers to the future of the Christian.[1] This has already been noted in connection with the passage Rom. 6.4 ff. But the usage there is corroborated at other points. We are said to be together with him in glory: 'joint-heirs with Christ; if so be that we suffer with him, that we be also glorified together' (Rom. 8.17); 'if we suffer, we shall also reign with him' (II Tim. 2.12); being raised up, we are to be made to 'sit together in heavenly places in Christ Jesus' (Eph. 2.6); and most significant of all: 'your life is hid with Christ in God.[2] When Christ who is our life shall appear, then shall ye also appear with him in glory' (Col. 3.3 f.). Our future standing is designated, not as in Christ, but characteristically as with Christ.

The pattern is thus discernible. In the days of the incarnation, men could be with Christ. As already said, the apostles are desig-

---

[1] Cf. the testimony of C. H. Dodd (*Romans*, 89), already quoted in Chapter I: 'Paul constantly uses *with Christ* of the future status of Christians, as distinct from their present state *in Christ*.'

[2] This sentence presents a particularly nice problem in Pauline prepositional usage—'with Christ', but 'in God'. It is perhaps simplest to construe it as referring both to the present (strictly 'in Christ') and to the future (strictly 'with Christ') stages of the Christian career. St Paul does not think it necessary to discriminate between the stages here, because in fact the Christian's life here and now is identifiable with his life hereafter: it is represented under the category of a *present* hiddenness which *will* be retracted.

nated as those who should be 'with him', and the candidates for the vacancy occasioned by the defection of Judas have to be qualified by their having 'companied with us all the time that the Lord Jesus went in and out among us' (Acts 1.21). It is the characteristic mark of these days that men could be with him. There follow the death at Calvary, the resurrection and the ascension; and at the far side of these moments in Christ's career, in which men can only be with him in so far as they are in Christ, there appears the expected consummation, when men are once again to be with him. In the present, God sees men as in virtue of their standing in Christ. When it comes to the last things, such is his efficacy, they stand with him. As Calvin puts it,[1] 'He entered [heaven] in our nature, and as it were in our names,' and consequently 'we now "sit together" with him "in heavenly places" (Eph. 2.6).' 'It is a source of peculiar consolation to hear that he . . . has already predestined us to participation with himself in the honour of sitting in judgment with him.'[2] In the present, God sees and deals with us as in Christ—it is the sphere of faith; in the eschatological future, we stand beside or with Christ—it is the sphere of sight (I Cor. 13.12).

Is this the clue which gives us understanding of that certain 'subordinationism' which is apparent in the New Testament witness to the office of the Son at the last, and to which H. R. Mackintosh[3] and others have drawn attention? What is the office whose discharge enables the Son at length to be 'himself subject to him that put all things under him' (I Cor. 15.28)? May we not understand it as representing men before the Father—the men whom by his work he assumes into himself, and who being made participant also in his risen life he represents 'in the heavenly places' here and now, the men also who when the last day comes will stand no longer in their Representative but beside their Advocate, no longer in Christ but with Christ? In rendering up his office to become 'subject', he is really rendering up those whom he undertook to benefit by his work; and as he renders us up, we are said to be with him rather than in him. And as he now pleads for us who stand in the presence of the Father, he being both Advocate and Judge (I John 2.1; Rom. 14.10; II Cor. 5.10), the stage is set for the final decision to be made upon us.

[1] *Inst.* 1.14.16.   [2] Op. cit. 1.14.18.
[3] *The Person of Jesus Christ*, Edinburgh 1913, 71 ff. The strain is recurrent and varied in the history of doctrine. It is of course both separable from Arian tendencies and congruous with homoousian principles.

5. *Universalism or particularism*

We are thus confronted by the perplexing question of men's final destiny. For whom in the last solemn day are things going to go well, and for whom ill? With greater precision since Christ really is Saviour, there will certainly be members of the first class; are there members of the second, to whom is apportioned eternal loss? Are we to come down on the side of universalism or of particularism?

The question is not answerable, any more than any other major question, by the citation of biblical passages. If 'God so loved the world' (John 3.16) can be read in favour of the universalist understanding, it can be offset by the synoptic dominical word that the ransom is for many (Matt. 20.28). But even these cited verses can be differently expounded: the first when it is pointed out that there is no guarantee of entire success for this love with which God loves the world; the second if the 'many' be interpreted as a denial of 'few' or 'none' rather than of 'all'. The only conclusion is that there is no simple solution to be found in isolated scriptural texts, for their witness is equivocal. On the other hand, and perhaps consequently, the anxious question raised here too often has a solution imposed upon it framed less by reflection than by sentimentality. A. E. Taylor is entirely justified when he declares[1] that the deliverances of mere 'good nature' are often in this connection at variance with ethical seriousness, and, we may add, with theological considerations also.

We must allow the course of the argument outlined in what has been said to lead us as far as it can. What Christ has contrived for us is something quite objective; to this position of high favour we are given access; and from it as vantage point faith and all the diverse 'fruit of the Spirit' spring. If what he does is isolated and more precisely characterized, we may further say that 'Christ dies for our sins' (I Cor. 15.3), that this is a completed work, and that men are neither able nor obliged to add anything to it. But if this is so, then what he has done applies to all men, and the universality of its application is really implicit in its completeness. If 'Christ Jesus came into the world to save sinners' (I Tim. 1.15), then his work is for all, 'for all have sinned, and come short of the glory of God' (Rom. 3.23). And if those for whom he died are thereby assumed into the status of being in Christ, then unbelievers and atheists have also been thus assumed.

[1] *The Faith of a Moralist*, London 1931, I, 330.

Does this, then, shut us up to universalism? The very complete-ness of Christ's work seems to imply its universality: all men are assumed by what he is through what he does to participation in him and are thereby made his beneficiaries. Does this mean that all men must be saved? The answer must be in the negative. To draw this conclusion is to go too fast. The insistence here laid upon the com-pleteness and universality of the work of Christ has not faced this question as stated. What it has done is to alter the terms in which the question must be formulated. Its usual formulation misunder-stands the nature of the decision that is asked of us. It is thought that the alternatives are that we either lay hold upon Christ and so become what we are not, or fail to lay hold upon him and so remain what we are. But to adopt this formulation would be to unlearn what has been said here about the character of the work of Jesus Christ, and once again our decision and choice would thrust them-selves into that undue prominence which is characteristic of those who have not fundamentally broken with Pelagianism and Syner-gism. The question has to be otherwise formulated. Properly expressed, the alternatives before us are: either that we be what we are or that we become what we are not. This formulation is quite different from the first. The first sinks back again into under-standing Christ as offering something which we have then to make our own; the second sees Christ as having conferred a real status upon us which we have to work out. The first, when all is said, has not rid itself of thinking of salvation anthropologically; the second sees it through and through as christological—the altogether splen-did work of him who 'while we were yet sinners, died for us' (Rom. 5.8). We are indeed 'sharing in God's work' (II Cor. 6.1, NEB), not in the sense that the work commences when God and we decide to begin it, but in the sense that to the work already wrought for and in us we say Amen, and humbly begin to work with him in the sphere to which he has admitted us.[1]

It is on these presuppositions that we can rightly address ourselves to the question raised by universalism. Universalism can mean either of two things: either that all will be saved, or that all cannot but be saved. About the first, it is surely right to say that we can have hope but not certainty. Here the considerations so forcibly

[1] The whole text corroborates what is being said here. 'Sharing in God's work, we urge this appeal upon you: you have received the grace of God; do not let it go for nothing' (NEB). St Paul is saying: God's grace is already yours; see to it that you do not render it vain.

expressed recently by H. H. Farmer[1] have their part to play. God's love 'never turns aside from or deserts any human person that he has made. . . . On the contrary, he seeks with undeviating patience and at any cost to bring every man back to that true personal life which is to be found only in fellowship with himself and in the doing of his will.'[2] It must be thought a grave reverse for God 'if vast numbers of persons are finally lost in some sort of hell, or (as some have suggested) by total annihilation'.[3] And clearly our hope is far more firmly founded if the pressure of God's relentless love is regarded as the continuation of a work already done for us in which we participate and from which we benefit, than when it is regarded as having to await the first stirrings of a man's apprehension and acceptance before its triumph can even begin.

But the second form in which universalism is held must be repudiated. It cannot be regarded as the clear witness of Scripture. At best it can then be only an implication, correct only if we have not only all the premises correct but also all the premises that are relevant. If anything is true about the religious situation as presented by Christianity, it is that great issues not yet finally decided are at stake, and will remain at stake until the last day. To deny this is to drain life of the meaning with which Christianity believes Christ to have invested it. If so, we cannot say all men must be saved, for this is to import into the whole matter a natural type of necessity which is as irrelevant as it is improper.

In what sense, then, may we say that the issue is still undecided, if in Christ it has already been decided for us? It is one thing to say that the issue at stake is an entirely open issue, quite dependent upon a choice in which the individual is wholly free. This is not what is maintained here. For it is quite another thing to say that God predetermines all in Jesus Christ, but with such a grace as is precisely not in the Augustinian sense irresistible. The possibility exists that men may be finally lost. How, then, is this possibility to be conceived? The cardinal error in Calvin's forbidding doctrine of *praedestinatio duplex* is that the decree to election and the decree to reprobation are in the last resort related in the same way to the will of God and equally subserve his glory. It is true that Calvin does recognize a certain asymmetry in the respective relations. For, while the final well-being of the elect is entirely dependent upon God and what he does for them in Jesus Christ, in the case of the final

---

[1] *God and Men*, London 1948, 134–51.   [2] Op. cit. 134.   [3] Op. cit. 144.

destiny of the reprobate there is interposed a factor other than the pure will of God, namely their unbelief, and this, however much it falls under the final disposition of God, is none the less their own responsibility. But this is not the asymmetry which is most important in the Christian faith. Despite all that he says about the infinite tenderness of God towards his children, Calvin never allows the scriptural testimony unreservedly to rule his thought, that God 'will have all men to be saved, and to come to the knowledge of the truth' (I Tim. 2.4), and he never regards this as definitive of the primary will of God. Yet precisely this is declared by the career of him whom God sent. Jesus Christ is crucified, dead and buried— he is reprobate. If that were all, or if that were all so far as Jesus Christ were concerned and another took his place as the declared elect of God, then we should have to think that God held election and reprobation in equilibrium. But it is not all, and he who is reprobate is also he that is raised again: Easter Day succeeds Good Friday. God shows his preference: his will is life and not death, election and not reprobation. Something is left behind and something remains: reprobation is cancelled, literally crossed out; and there remains only victorious election. This asymmetry of relation to God finds its correlate (in terms already used) in a contrariety in our relation to Christ. He suffers reprobation in order that we may not ourselves have to undergo it; he is the subject of election, 'the firstborn among many brethren' (Rom. 8.29), and we in Christ enjoy this with him. This is the point which Barth makes with unwearying emphasis.[1] 'The decision and act of man are, of course, required by the direction given and revealed in Jesus Christ. But the requirement of the divine direction is based on the fact that in Jesus Christ man has already been put in the place and kingdom of peace with God. His decision and act, therefore, can consist only in obedience to the fact that he begins and does not cease to breathe in this place and kingdom, that he follows the decision already made and the act already accomplished by God, confirming them in his own human decision and act; that he for his part chooses what has already been chosen and actualised for him.' The revelation of God's love 'embraces *realiter* both the world and the community, non-Christians and Christians. But the knowledge and proclamation of it is a matter only for the Christian community.'

The nature of the dreadful possibility of final loss thus becomes

[1] *Church Dogmatics* IV/1 100, 103.

a little clearer. It consists in a cleaving to that option against which God has set his face, a persistence in the No which God utters at the cross instead of the Yes of the resurrection which succeeds and supersedes the cross. This is what Barth means when, in a no doubt difficult conception, he declares that 'the choice of the godless man is void'.[1] The wheel has thus, in a manner of speaking, come full cycle. At an earlier point it was said that man is represented in Scripture as capable both of being and of not being man. This 'existential' ambiguity (if the phrase is permissible) persists even in the 'new creature' which he is 'in Christ' (II Cor. 5.17). As in the beginning he is properly in fellowship with God and yet embraces improper manhood, so now too, when he is remade in Christ in proper manhood, he can turn away from this reconstituted manhood and become what he is not. This reconstituted nature has not the same instability as the former which was lost. For in the case of the earlier, the road to improper being was stopped by a divine command; in the case of the new, the road to improper being is stopped by a cross. Here we are faced not so much by paradox as by surd. The choice of such a crossed-out road can only be the product of evil; and evil cannot be rationalized or rendered intelligible, for otherwise it would have the same relation to the will of God as does good. And this is not a Christian belief.

Here no doubt there will arise the question as to how within the terms used we are to account for the fact that X is a Christian and Y not, that X has faith while Y lacks it. It is a question that often recurs[2] and not infrequently with unhappy results. Of course the question is an anxious one and cannot simply be dismissed. We can hardly be heedless of the final outcome, indifferent whether God's grace can be finally repudiated, and unconcerned about how it comes about that someone whom we ourselves know appears quite unable to accept this grace. The temptation is very strong at this point to take the matter out of God's hands and to fall back on the simple answer that it all depends upon our accepting or refusing this grace. Yet Calvin is surely right here when he points out[3] that St Paul must also have been aware of this simple solution and yet steadfastly repudiates it. Why, asks Calvin, does he take the hard way out of the difficulty? Manifestly because he did not believe

---

[1] *Church Dogmatics* II/2 306.
[2] From the time of St Augustine (e.g. *Ep.* 105 to Sixtus [*Ep.* 194 in Migne 33]) onwards.
[3] See *Concerning the Eternal Predestination of God*, §V.3.

that any other solution was right. The simple solution is in error because it fails to see that, since faith is the gift of God and not man's contribution to his own salvation, unfaith must equally, though by no means similarly, be related to the will of God. In other words, the divine predestination is at stake. If what has here been said is accepted, we ought not to allow a subsequent query, however difficult and anxious, to drive us to conclusions that must immediately throw doubt upon the truth of the doctrine.

Does what has been said 'regard the primal decision of God as having so settled the issue of human destiny that the significance of a human Yes or No to God's claim has now scarcely a meaning'?[1] The answer must certainly be in the negative. To think it does so only shows that the idea of similarity or even identity between God's predestination and all kinds of determinism has not really been discarded. At this point it has crept back again, and deterministic concepts supplant what is properly meant by predestination. Then certainly the human Yes and No can only be regarded as meaningless—but only then. Within divine predestination Yes and No retain their absolutely important meaning—for to say No is to repudiate the status which Christ has bestowed upon men, and to say Yes is to acknowledge it with all that this implies.

If on the other hand the question signifies doubt not so much about the meaning of the human Yes and No as about their possibility, the answer has to be rather differently framed, though the terms remain much the same. How does X say Yes and Y No? The answer is that the possibility is there simply because of the predetermination of God. It is because of what Jesus Christ has done that a man can say Yes. How could he say Yes in his own power and on his own responsibility? how could he say Yes unless Jesus had already raised him to the status and place where alone it is possible and also requisite for him to say Amen to what has been done for him? For this he was predetermined by God. But he is not thereby determined to do so. Predetermination is the defined field in which men retain and do not forfeit their responsibility and individuality against all encroachments, the field therefore in which it is possible to say No as it is also possible to say Yes. When, however, the question is put in the form Why?, we cannot even go as far as this. To the question why X says Yes, there is no answer—no answer, that is, outside Jesus Christ himself; and a man says Yes

[1] See C. S. Duthie, 'Ultimate Triumph', *Scottish Journal of Theology*, XIV 2, 1961, 166.

simply because Jesus Christ is Jesus Christ and shows himself to be who and what he is. In the widest possible sense, 'bread-and-butter Christians' are not Christians at all; or as St Augustine more academically says: *illuminatio nostra participatio Verbi*. The question why Y says No has similarly no answer, but for quite dissimilar reasons. If we could answer it, we should be bringing evil into the class of understandable things and giving it a reality equal to that of the grace of God; and this, as we have seen, we cannot and may not do.

Is the negative choice ever actually made? Men have by the grace of God in Jesus Christ been admitted to a status in which they are in Christ, for their liberation from reprobation and their participation in life. Will there at the last be any who 'contract out' of this divinely contrived and bestowed status? To this question we have no certain answer. Legend tells us that Henry II of England 'on his death-bed deliberately blasphemed God in order to ensure his own damnation. "Since thou," he is made to say, "hast taken from me the thing I most delight in, Le Mans, I will deprive thee of the thing in me thou hast most delight in, my soul." '[1] Did this ever happen? Perhaps no historian will venture to say that it did and no theologian that it could not. For this is a possibility, and has all the reality of a possibility, and this makes it different from something which just is not. We may certainly hope that no one will make this possibility actually his own and so embrace the 'great refusal'. Yet the possibility stands before us men, cancelled out as it is by the sign of the cross. It is constitutive of the grandeur as also of the peril of the existence of those whom God in the work of creation made for fellowship with himself and in the work of salvation has taken to be in Christ. This being so, we should do well to pay heed to the words of A. E. Taylor:[2] 'There is just one man, of the many whom I have known, about whom I feel it salutary not to be over-sanguine, myself.' The possibility is there, and it is individually ours, to set at nought what Jesus Christ has wrought for us already in his person and by his work.

Therefore

> *quaerens me sedisti lassus,*
> *redemisti crucem passus;*
> *tantus labor non sit cassus.*[3]

Or in the words of Scripture: 'work out your own salvation with fear and trembling' (Phil. 2.12).

---

[1] A. E. Taylor, *The Faith of a Moralist* I, 167.   [2] Op. cit. I, 331.
[3] From *Dies Irae* by (?) Thomas of Celano.

INDEX OF NAMES AND SUBJECTS

Wellhausen, Julius, 53 n. 2.
Wesley, John, 112
Williams, N. P., 48, 49, 106 ff.,
  114 n. 1, 115 nn. 2, 3, 118

with Jesus, with Christ, 14 f., 133,
  135 ff.

Zeph, Max, 42 f.

INDEX OF BIBLICAL REFERENCES

OLD TESTAMENT

Genesis
1   39 f.
1.26   34, 40
1.26 ff.   44 n. 3, 46 n. 3
1.27   36
2.9   45 n. 9
5.1   36
9.5–7   45 n. 1
9.6   36
22.1   88
39.20   34

Exodus
21.29, 34   34

Leviticus
19.2   110

Job
1.6   45 n. 6
5.20 f.   46 n. 1
10.7   45 n. 3
30.15   45 n. 10
38.36   37

Psalms
8.5   45 n. 1

19   39
22.1   88
40.6   73 n. 2
95.6   64
103   39

Isaiah
19.4   34
40.13   37

Jeremiah
10.23   46

NEW TESTAMENT

Matthew
4.19   86
4.23   85
5–7   85
5.48   85, 110
6.24   75
7.24–27   75
9.35   85
11.29   86
12.48   88
13.58   103
14.35   122
16.15   76
16.16 ff.   104, 116
16.21   122
16.24   86
18.20   14
19.16–22   76
20.28   88, 134, 138
21.23   85
23.55   85
24.25   85
26.24, 45   122
27.46   88
28.20   85

Mark
3.14   14

3.34   88
8.35   75
10.45   88
14.50   103
15.34   88

Luke
7.50   103
13.10   85
18.13   64
19.10   88
22.14   122
22.22   119, 122
22.53   122
23.5   85
24.26 f.   122
24.51   64

John
1.3   35 n. 1
1.17   39
3.16   138
6.31   73 n. 2
6.41   64
6.44   111, 114
6.50, 58   64
7.30   122
8.20   122

8.42   73
8.43   70
9.4   122
12.23, 27   122
13–17   85
13.1   122
13.15   87
14.12   73
15.4   14
15.14 f.   88
15.27   14
16.10   73
17.1, 4   122
17.24   15
20.17   133
20.31   68

Acts
1.9   64
1.21   137
2.11   26
2.23   122, 133
5.25   26
9.2   11
10.45   11
11.26   9
14.2   11
15.13   11